Ever

The Growing Co.

by
Jeff Wynn and Louise Wynn

Everyone is a Believer

The Growing Convergence of Science and Religion

by

Jeff Wynn and Louise Wynn

Cover Image: Veil Nebula (NGC 6992) - NASA, ESA, and The Hubble Heritage Team (STScI/AURA)

Kindle Direct Publishing

http://www.ldsscientist.com/

ISBN: 978-1-79-560776-6

2019

Preface

Have you ever tasted a neutrino? Felt one? Then why would you ever believe that every night as you sleep, 500 trillion neutrinos pass from your floor through your body every second? You'd have to have faith in something, right? Consider Wolfgang Pauli and Enrico Fermi, well-known physicists in the 1930's, trying to understand beta decay with their primitive equipment. An atomic nucleus, for reasons only it could possibly understand, suddenly emitted an electron and changed its atomic number by one – and the atom became a different element. The mass appeared to be conserved in this radioactive decay, and charge was definitely conserved, but spin – angular momentum – was <u>not</u> conserved. Fermi believed in the Law of Conservation of Angular Momentum, because he had never before seen it violated. Together he and Pauli thought and argued and eventually proposed that there must be another particle emitted at the same time – but one that had no mass (huh?) and no charge... and was *spinning*. Eduardo Amaldi, in a conversation with Fermi (both Italian), proposed calling this unknown and unobserved thing a neutrino – a tiny neutral thing. Now, *that* is an exercise in faith. It wasn't until 1956 that, by very indirect means, the existence of neutrinos was first tentatively verified by Clyde Cowan and Frederick Reines, resulting in the 1995 Nobel Prize almost 40 years later (Cowan had died, so only Reines received the prize, which he shared with Stanford's Martin L. Perl [Nobel Prize, 1995]). This is just one of innumerable examples of how faith drives science.

Science, religion, and philosophy share many elements, but one is more important than all the rest: they are all efforts by imperfect humans to understand what is true. By "true" we mean what is *correct* – something that when tested can be verified to be that very specific something. You might, for instance, wonder if the label on your milk carton is true... or mostly true. On the largest scale of importance, however, are the correct answers to these three questions: (1) Why are we on this planet, (2) Why we are able to even think about it, and (3) What comes next? This book surveys many of the places where science, religion, and philosophy are rapidly beginning to intersect as they seek to answer these and other questions.

In an age where each of these three approaches to truth has become a religion for even some who would deny they are religious, we show that the three approaches are all converging on the same, larger

Truth. All three approaches, to a surprising degree, depend on exercising faith in one form or another. Moreover, science and religion almost always involve _indirect_ proof that anything is true. You have never seen or tasted a neutrino, an atom, the weak nuclear force, the Southwest Washington Crustal Conductor, or the Holy Ghost.

In these short chapters we separate science from technology, with which it is often conflated. We discuss the apparent successes and the imperfect and very human shortcomings of science, and we do this from an insider's point of view (we are both professional scientists, but we also are "adherents to a faith tradition"). You may have already noticed that science as taught in college is often quite different from real science as practiced on laboratory benches and in observatories. An awful lot of science is just plain muddling – imperfect humans trying to get some measurement to repeat, to get a series of data points to fit a mathematical model, to line up on a regression curve.

One problem is that most measurements we make in the laboratory (or in the jungle or in outer space) pick up the signal being sought, but also noise – a lot of noise. There is noise in everything – and too much of science consists of trying to draw some significance from what ultimately is just random or systemic noise. It's almost always easier (and always shorter) to explain science in mathematics rather than in English. However, if you try to use math and fit a regression curve to noise, you get bad science: non-reproducible junk science. You're putting lipstick on a ghost pig.

Like science, religion and philosophy also have human limits and frailties. This starts with the rather fundamental question: how can we ever even know if an idea or concept is true in the first place? Can we test it? Yes – but like scientists, we must always begin with a few basic assumptions, and one of these implicitly is that we are not on this planet by accident – that there is a reason for all this. Scientists, whether atheists, agnostics, or theists, all have to operate under certain basic assumptions. There are assumptions behind everything: scientists must accept the basic physics laws of the universe and the anthropic principle, even though they do not know why they exist in the first place. They must also build on previous discoveries. The reason for accepting all these underlying assumptions is we just can't keep inventing the wheel over and over again. We have to build on something that we are confident in, even if we don't understand it. Some things we will never be able to measure or prove, such as what preceded the Big Bang, and why the anthropic principle just IS.

We have referred to the Troika for seeking the Ultimate Truth as science, philosophy, and religion. We will discuss philosophy only briefly, and only to make certain crucial points about what is science and what is *not* science. In part this is because philosophy is a huge field of study in its own right that neither of us is well grounded in, though we have both studied it. In part, we have noticed that philosophy is constantly evolving – its history abundantly shows this.

However, certain elements of philosophy are crucially important, especially logic and the philosophy of science, because philosophers like Karl Popper have forced scientists to be honest. If not for these philosophers, we would all be squatting around campfires beating rocks and discussing String Theory until the Sun goes nova.

By the way, what could history possibly have to do with science and religion? Well, if you didn't know that until 1965 scientists were promoting cigarette smoking as a way to improve digestion, you might think that science is perfect. Science history makes it abundantly clear, however, that like all other human endeavors, science moves forward and learns new things with stutter-steps and lots of failures – just as all human beings do. People who put their faith and adoration into science thus do so at great long-term personal peril.

Many people may be surprised to learn that religion, like good science, is something that is testable, and that many people have in fact tested it. Both authors fit in this latter category, and we consider ourselves very fortunate (the secular word for "blessed") because of the guidance this implies. Because we both consider ourselves part of the larger Family of Man (the secular expression for "Children of the same God"), we feel it is incumbent upon us to share these observations. We are scientists. We are your brother and sister.

~ ~ ~ ~ ~

Interestingly, one Christian denomination is apparently unique in that its adherents also clearly understand that they do <u>not</u> have all the elements of truth, only that they are on the correct path to get there. We have written records, for instance, that fully one-third of the Book of Mormon was sealed and unavailable to Joseph Smith to translate. It is no accident that there is such a great emphasis in the Church of Jesus Christ of Latter-Day Saints on gaining and steadily adding to an advanced education. There is transparently no fear of learning something faith shaking here. The whole idea is to seek the truth, and that brooks no close-mindedness, no certitude, no elimination of anything *a priori* – including denying the existence of a transcendent or even an imminent God.

Please note that this book does not attempt to prove the truth of the Book of Mormon (more in a subsequent chapter on why that misses the point), nor does it try to prove the "correctness" of the Church of Jesus Christ of Latter-day Saints. It does, however, offer interesting and sometimes startling observations about convergence with science that will draw the attention of any honest, open-minded scientist or, indeed, any interested reader. Some key points:

- Scientists – whether believers, agnostics, or atheists – all must start from basic *a priori* assumptions, and in multiple ways they exercise a faith functionally indistinguishable from people adhering to a faith tradition. One obvious corollary: everyone is a believer.

- It is not only possible to be a scientist and a believer in God, but, from the authors' perspective, you cannot honestly separate the two, nor peremptorily discard one for the other on the basis of incomplete information (or deliberately ignored information).

- For a number of reasons, it is probably not wise to even attempt to scientifically prove that God exists, or that a particular religion is true, or that there is an afterlife. Science just isn't built for this. *But there sure are a lot of strong hints out there.*

- Science is evolving and incomplete, and some modern "science" (like the "multiverse theory") is not even science. By its nature, however, science is inherently unable to prove or disprove any religious beliefs, and philosophy can only suggest possible answers.

- Some of the science described in this book was up to date at the time of writing, but the evolving nature of science is such that some parts will inevitably be superseded by something newer. *This just proves several of our points on scientific impermanence, scientific evolution – and convergence.*

- Philosophy is replete with ideas, but these have evolved with time – nothing seems anchored with respect to the really fundamental questions like *"Where did we come from?"*, *"Why are we here?"*, and *"Where are we going?"* Moreover, most ideas in philosophy cannot be proven – can't be tested – but philosophy can at least help us learn how to think more coherently. Logic and falsifiability are aspects of philosophy that have definitely helped science become better at sorting out truth from non-truth, and science from meta-philosophy, in the past two centuries.

- Science, philosophy, and religion are nevertheless each rapidly converging on a much larger truth, and we believe this is no accident. In fact, this convergence seems to be accelerating, starting early in the 19th Century. A 23-yr-old with a 3rd grade education first opened the door in 1828.

NOTE: There is some repetition in the following chapters. This is because we've deliberately tried to make each chapter short, self-contained and comprehensible, and accessible to everyone. One of the authors (the physicist) reads slowly, and he understands that there are others who appreciate short, fun chapters to read where they actually learn something new:
Something True.

Table of Contents

Introduction

We are not the first scholars or scientists who acknowledge membership in the Church of Jesus Christ of Latter-Day Saints. Nor are we the first to have published books or papers on science and religion (Nibley, 1967; Eyring, 1967, 1972, 1983; Sorenson, 1984, 1985, 1992; Baer, 1986; Paul, 1992; Lyon et al., 1994; Kowallis, 1999; Stephens et al., 2001; Givens, 2002; Jordan, 2003; Lewis, 2013; Interpreter Foundation, 2013, Hamblin, 2015; among many excellent others). So, what could possibly justify yet another book on science and religion for members of this Church – and for our friends who don't consider themselves religious, or who believe that being religious makes it impossible to be a scientist or a scholar? The answer: What we present here is different – this book demonstrates a *growing convergence* between good science and true religion (true religion being, like good science, defined as something that can survive testing). There is also in this book a great deal of new scientific, geographic, and linguistic evidence not available to previous authors. We show how this increase in knowledge enriches both our scientific and spiritual life, just as a firm grounding in true religion can make us better scientists.

In the eighth chapter of Third Nephi in the Book of Mormon there is a vivid description of a series of events that befell the inhabitants of part of the New World at the time of the death of Christ. This narrative is interesting in a number of ways, starting with its remarkable specificity, including a precise date (in the local calendar) for when the destructive events took place and how long they lasted. The narrative also includes a number of elements that were not understood by early Book of Mormon readers, including a huge storm carrying catastrophic destruction with it, extensive lightning, massive ground shaking, the entire face of the land being altered, and several references to a terrible "vapor of darkness."

The Book of Mormon was first published in March 1830. Anyone who had read it before May 18, 1980, then, was riveted by the descriptions emerging of the catastrophic eruption of Mount St Helens in Washington State (Lipman and Mullineaux, 1991). More than 150 years earlier, the Book of Mormon gave a description of lightning associated with a Plinian-style volcanic eruption – rising volcanic ash dragging vast amounts of electrical charge up into the stratosphere. Here also were vivid descriptions of a "vapor of darkness" – volcanic glass in the form of lung-choking ash – suffocating people, snuffing campfires, and blacking out and shutting down central Washington State at mid-day. There were also descriptions of enormous changes to the regional topography, including the largest landslide in recorded human history, as a mountain was sheared off and valleys filled in, obliterating over 140 square miles of once pristine forest north of the volcano.

Joseph Smith dictated the 522 pages of the Book of Mormon in roughly 53 days, without going back and revising the text. But Joseph had never seen a volcano, knew nothing of plate tectonics and Central American geology, and had barely more than a 3rd grade education. He had no idea what the Frankincense Trail was, and he had no idea what Egyptian name-construction rules were 2,600 years ago, or for that matter, anything about the ancient Semitic language cognates and linguistic structures found in the Uto-Aztecan language group. Joseph had no knowledge of military logistics, prisoner management, military fortifications, nor had he (or anyone else at the time) any clue about a 2,500-yr-old Hebrew poetic style now called chiasmus. These things were not taught in the third grade in western New York in the early 1800's.

There are a number of rather startling cases like this in the Bible, too. Vivid descriptions of processes were not understood for millennia, but they have been verified or understood decades or even centuries later by archaeology. For example, the story of Noah's flood may be explained by the filling of the Black Sea basin roughly 7,000 years ago (Ryan et al., 1997). There are other examples: Jericho lies on a transform fault much like the San Andreas, for instance, and excavations show many levels of devastated walls and structures. King Solomon's Ophir gold mines turn out to be 852 (yes, the US Geological Survey has counted them) small ancient mines in the western Arabian Shield (Smith and Blank, 1979; Wynn and Blank, 1979; Leach, 2014).

In the last several decades, astronomers and cosmologists have gleaned information about the singularity that began our universe 13.8 billion years ago, now universally called the Big Bang. There is newly available information about the enormous black hole in the center of our galaxy, about vacuum energy, about the outer bounds of the universe, about dark matter, and recently even dark energy. Yet William W. Phelps, a personal scribe to Joseph Smith, wrote a hymn in 1835 that appears to understand these things, and alludes to them in startling detail, lacking only the specialized modern vocabulary (Church of Jesus Christ of Latter-Day Saints, Hymn 284, *If You Could Hie to Kolob*).

As a geophysicist, a recovering atheist and convert to the Church of Jesus Christ, Jeff has always been interested in the links between science, religion, and philosophy. Raised in the Church by devout descendants of

Mormon pioneers, Louise grew up wondering if she should accept the faith of her ancestors just because they believed. She wondered why teachers and relatives offered unscientific and sometimes even unreasonable answers to her questions about scriptural and doctrinal issues; and why their answer was sometimes, "Just because." And even, once, "If you keep asking these questions, it keeps you from being a good Christian." Being a questioner is built into both of us, and we have both actively explored many other fields of science, finding answers in fields within and outside our initial specialties. This has led to peer-reviewed scientific publications in archaeology, astrophysics, biology, ecology, geology, geophysics, hydrology, linguistics, mineral resources assessments, ocean engineering, and volcanology (some of these are included in References).

We all teach our children correct principles as they grow up (to the extent that we understand these principles ourselves), but these children must exercise their own free agency. Later we may think of things we wish we had also addressed. Why didn't we tell them how to bore down to the truth behind the lies, the hidden agendas, on some website? Why didn't we tell them more – like how we routinely use prayer and inspiration to avoid research dead-ends and thus improve our success as scientists? In a world where science has become a religion for some, why didn't we show our kids the areas of science that still have huge gaps in understanding, the currently fashionable but profoundly non-scientific hypotheses, the gaping holes in scientific belief-and-self-rationalization systems, the vast false content in the Internet? Most people on this planet are seeking answers to questions that sometimes they can only vaguely even frame. For science and religion both, getting these answers requires accepting many things on faith (a priori) first. Contrary to popular thinking, as much faith and belief are exercised in science as in religion. Some but not all atheists get upset at hearing this; however, it's true. When you get right down to it, everyone is a believer in one way or another.

This book was primarily written for members of the Church of Jesus Christ of Latter-Day Saints, sometimes called Mormons, but it is intended for a much wider audience: to all those who instinctively understand that information derived from science and religion are *both* incomplete and are *not* mutually exclusive. This book is for people who instinctively sense that there are other sources of knowledge besides scientific experiments. This book is for all those who are interested in the intersection of science and religion with a larger Truth, which we spell with a capital "T" to indicate that it doesn't continue to evolve, that it's unchangeable. And hey – what are these Church of Jesus Christ people onto that I don't see? Why do they put such a high priority on advanced education? Why do surveys consistently show them to be happier, better educated, and living longer than the general population? Can everything true really be gathered into one great whole?

Science and true religion really are converging, and the speed in some areas is breathtaking. We're just starting to see where this is all heading, and the door was first opened in 1820.

Perspectives

Alternative ways of looking at life

Man lying on his death bed: *"I should have bought more crap."*
– Lewis (cartoonist)
"I always wanted to be somebody. Now I see I should have been more specific."
– Lily Tomlin (comedian)
"I desire to go to Hell and not to Heaven. In the former I shall enjoy the company of popes, kings, and princes, while in the latter are only beggars, monks, and apostles."
– Niccolo Machiavelli (political advisor)
"I owe Asclepius a rooster."
– Last words of Socrates (philosopher)
"It's my turn to take a leap into the darkness."
– Last words of Thomas Hobbes (philosopher).

Have you thought:
- What you want to be remembered for?
- Whom you want to be remembered by?
- What *will* be remembered about you 50 years from now – that is, what *really* counts?

A friend, a member of the Church, recounted a conversation he once held with a non-member friend who was married to a Church member. After a difficult business confrontation, Dave complimented his friend on his ability to keep a cool head through the process.

The friend replied, "Well, I just think, 'Will this have an impact five or ten years from now?' If the answer is no, it really is not important enough to worry about."

Dave asked, "What about 100 years? Do you think about that?"

The friend answered "No, why?"

Dave said, "Well, when you do, you will be a member of the Church of Jesus Christ."

Atheists TOO

We're all atheists. And we're all believers.

As an eleven-year-old, I began to notice a problem. I reasoned: If the Tooth Fairy, the Easter Bunny, and Santa Claus were not real, what *else* were the adults telling me that might also not be real? What about God? And so I became an agnostic, although I didn't know the word. By the time I was 12 my sense of betrayal had hardened into an amorphous anger, and I became acutely critical of everything adults told me, trying to outline the boundaries between truth and kindly intended adult fiction.

I had careful arguments with the Catholic nuns in my elementary school about Limbo (where, according to Catholic dogma, unbaptized infants and children are trapped for all eternity), and about papal infallibility. Those arguments with the nuns were "careful" in the sense that, if we were perceived to be arguing with – sassing – a nun, we would be quickly beaten. And we really were beaten. I remember being slapped several times so hard that it set me staggering, and always having bruises on my hands from being whacked with wooden pointers and rulers.

I learned altogether too much about the history of the Papacy. As a twelve-year-old I was given a homework assignment to research the life of a Pope. At the local library I got permission to go into the "adult stacks" and pull a volume at random of the history of the Catholic Church, and so, randomly, I picked one. I learned he was the son of a Pope, had fathered a subsequent Pope (with his sister), and was stricken with paralysis and died while committing fornication with a mistress (McCabe, 1939; McBrien, 1997; Maxwell-Stuart, 1997). The Vicar of Christ? A direct link in the line of authority from Peter?

As a result of all that I became pretty sure that the faith my Mom had raised me in was hooey. My Mom still made me go to church, though, so for three more years I was a Catholic Atheist Altar Boy. However, I never said this to her face, nor to the nuns, nor later to the Christian Brothers who taught us at Garces Junior High School. THEY could hit you so hard that you would hit the wall first, then slide down to the floor. By this time, I had learned those words "agnostic" and "atheist." Still, I could wear the cool cassock (robes), light and put out candles, ring bells loudly, and sometimes even sneak a taste of some of the wine.

For 10 years, then, I was an atheist. By the time I entered college I was a militant, abrasive atheist. I held the belief that if I couldn't see something with my own eyes, or derive it from Maxwell's equations, I wouldn't believe it. This is a classic example of being determinedly self-limiting – self-blinded, excluding evidence. By the way, excluding evidence is a Really Bad Thing in science – it's generally considered inexcusable, in fact. It's called "cherry-picking."

Many atheists now, like me then, don't accept the fact that there might be routes other than scientific experiment to gaining knowledge. Many atheists... but not all. As an example of these other routes to truth, however, I would note Einstein's "Gedankenexperiment" (thought experiment) that led to his multiply-verified special relativity and general relativity, so well proven by now with experimental evidence that they are no longer called "theories." I would also note the famous manner in which Pauli and Fermi postulated the neutrino decades before there was evidence to prove it, even indirectly. *They had faith.*

Many of my friends still subscribe to the atheist tradition, and we use here the word "tradition," in the same way that non-religious individuals refer to "religious traditions." However, they don't like being called an atheist – it has negative connotations, more so in some countries than in others. No, we don't understand that, either – atheists for the most part are just trying to be honest. However, atheist organizations cannot pin down Neil DeGrasse Tyson to even admit he's an atheist; he tries very hard to avoid that label, because it isn't helpful to his marketing. In some places and times, like Voltaire's France, being an atheist was fashionable. However, if you wish to enter Saudi Arabia, and you identify yourself as an atheist, you will not get a visa (they do ask). In fact, it is so *NOT* OK to be an atheist there that a Saudi who declared himself an atheist could be beheaded unless he publicly recanted.

Therefore, many of us atheists called ourselves "skeptics." This provided camouflage – you couldn't quite pin us down, while we could stand back, in a passive-aggressive way, and demand that people from a faith tradition prove things to *us*. It's a classic "Heads I win, tails you lose" way to load the argument up front. I have to admit that I used this one a lot. I wasn't above using ridicule to embarrass devout Christian friends who were scientists. Atheists have at least one thing in common with members of the Church of Jesus Christ of Latter-Day Saints (aka Mormons): they both are seeking the honest truth.

As atheists we also called ourselves "humanists" – in part to allay accusations that without religion we had no morals, but in part to also put us on the side of the "humans" on the planet. Who could object to that? As part of this, we argued that religious wars were the reason for most of the suffering and misery of humanity. Therefore, religions must be bad.

The problem with this approach is that it overlooks some of the most basic evidence of human history. Almost all conflict has been political (to gain power) or xenophobic (fear of outsiders) at its core. Attackers just used religion as a cover to justify the atrocities that almost all human beings know to be wrong. The Islamic State in Iraq and Syria is a classic example of this. They call themselves "Islamic" but are rejected by 99% of the Muslim world as false Muslims, violators of the core precepts of the Qur'an. They also murder Muslims almost exclusively. Faith-based, indeed.

Oddly, I don't think that anyone ever counted how many human beings were killed by three atheist regimes in the 20th Century. I can count Pol Pot (about 2 million), Josef Stalin (estimates generally exceed 20 million), and Mao Tse-Dung (estimates of the people killed during the Great Proletarian Cultural Revolution alone are up to 70 million). These deaths in the 20th Century exceed the deaths of all so-called "religious" wars in the previous millennium.

By the time I was 22, I was a "Mormon" – a member of the Church of Jesus Christ of Latter-day Saints. Wait – *what*?!?? How did that happen?

It happened because I began having problems again, this time with the logic (or lack thereof) of my thought system – my belief tradition – as an atheist. It was a problem of assumptions, of voids, and of functionally parallel belief frameworks. Atheism was just another religion, but it had no explanations. We have a cartoon on our refrigerator: two young men in white shirts have given a pamphlet to a man at his front door. "But this is blank," says the man. "We're atheists," replies one of the young men.

I think most of us would agree that people from a faith tradition have a belief framework. By that I mean that they accept some basic premises: for instance, that God exists, that our existence has a purpose. From these premises, everything both good and bad in their life experience can then be more or less understood. Our improbable human existence can be explained, pain and suffering can be explained, a reward system is laid out, and what happens when we die more or less inevitably follows.

However, atheists – like me once – also have a belief framework. Like the religious belief framework, it begins with certain unprovable assumptions, one of which is that God *doesn't* exist. The corollary is that the universe just sort of magically (with a Big Bang) came into existence. This can be argued with just as much basis, with just as much evidence, as a belief in God. Also, atheists assume the physical laws of the universe just exist, and can't be explained. As an atheist I never tried to jump off a building, because I accepted gravity as a fundamental physical law. That's a fancy way of saying I wasn't *that* stupid. (Or that I had faith.)

Another basic assumption that we atheists built on is that the Anthropic Principle (outlined in a subsequent chapter of that name) is just a lucky accident. Twenty-six physical constants all line up to values within a few percent of what is required in order for life to exist in this universe. "Lucky" actually fails to express the improbability adequately. Try multiplying two percent (0.02) by itself twenty-six times. It's *that* improbable. A common argument to explain these amazing multiplicative coincidences is that our universe is one of an infinite number of parallel universes – the multiverse. Ours just happened to be the one that had all the constants line up just right. Ummm... then where did all the energy and matter come from to make all these infinite universes? And while we're at it, can anyone test for a multiverse? Not even remotely (by definition everything else is a different universe and is un-reachable and un-testable), but there are a lot of highly educated people who still believe in this.

They have faith.

Atheism has prophets – the guardians and promulgators of the Ain't-no-God belief framework – who also write books. For reasons that escape me as a former atheist, some of these are even proselytizing atheists – preachers. I suspect this doesn't make sense to you either – on several levels (for instance, why would they even *care?*). I think this proselytizing may have a lot to do with seeking fame, with craving attention. Some of it may come from the human desire to have fellow-believers and even – especially – followers. Atheism also comes with temples and idols – the Large Hadron Collider comes to mind. I have a book on my shelf in which a theoretical physicist appears to be worshipping this human construct. It's gold-plated, too (Randall, 2005).

Finally, there's the Big Bang. There is abundant evidence that all matter and energy in our universe suddenly exploded into existence from a tiny point about 13.8 billion years ago. What triggered this? What preceded it? Like the anthropic principle, this constitutes what I call a void – something that I couldn't understand or explain – *so as an atheist I ignored it.* By age 20, I found myself ignoring more and more voids, and I was growing increasingly uncomfortable with my basic assumptions. I felt increasingly dishonest.

Like many others, I conflated science with atheism. As I mentioned earlier, I accepted as reality only those things I could sense or test physically, and as a budding scientist I thought that was the only intellectually honest path. I hadn't seen anything that I could consider a proof in the existence of an imminent God (a God who answers prayers, and cares about His individual creations), so I didn't want to waste time thinking about it. This approach may actually fall into the domain of agnosticism. Some atheists and most agnostics will readily admit that the vastness and order of the universe argues at least for the existence of a transcendent God (a Being who started this vast universe, but who could care less about some puny, late-arrival sentient creatures on an average planet in the outer fringes of a smallish galaxy). This way of thinking is actually being more honest, in my view: because no one can explain the reason for the physical laws, the Big Bang, nor the Anthropic Principle. Arguing for a multiverse is NOT an explanation – it's just another belief system, because it's un-testable and thus unscientific.

I began looking again at the belief systems behind faith traditions. I searched widely. Eventually, I came across the Church of Jesus Christ of Latter-Day Saints. They had a belief system that was internally consistent and didn't require me to believe one thing on Sunday and something else during the rest of the week. There were no huge voids I was expected to ignore. They were very open about there being some unanswered questions; one-third of the Book of Mormon was sealed by metal bands against immediate translation, for instance. *However, I learned that we were expected to seek and could get answers for ourselves – if we were willing to expend personal energy to get them.* I found the fact that we are actually encouraged to get answers truly startling – and profoundly exhilarating. True science and true religion should both encourage us to explore, and endeavor to find answers to things we don't yet understand.

What struck me most, however, was that there was no fear of science, no fear of education among the members of this Church – and they showed me a way to prove it all was correct.

It was testable.

Pascal's Wager

Wanna make a bet on God?

During the Enlightenment in 18th Century France, when agnosticism and atheism were fashionable among the intellectuals of the time, Voltaire and other contemporaries noted that the brilliant mathematician Blaise Pascal was an observant Catholic.

When asked, Pascal observed that there were just two possibilities:

1. God exists.

2. God does NOT exist.

As a precursor to the philosophy of pragmatism, Pascal contended that it was better to be a faithful Catholic than an agnostic or atheist. He explained that in the case that God exists and you do what He expects, you win. In the case that God does not exist, and you attend your church services and do the other things the church tells you He expects, you gain social benefits in a support system that exists in virtually all religions. Like insurance, it buys you peace of mind. In either case you win. This was the first formal use of decision theory, by the way (Connor, 2006).

As Pascal put it:

"If reason cannot be trusted, it is a better wager to believe in God than not."

Of course, there are some glaring holes in this logic:

What if God exists and (of course) realizes that you are only making a decision-tree bet – in effect gaming Him?

What if God exists, but he's not the God you have been worshiping?

Well, then, how does one know?

There are several possible answers here:

1. *"By their fruit ye shall know them"* – who seem to be happiest, to have the best-raised children who contribute to society, who live longest (you'll need to do a statistical average here)?

2. If you're a member of the Church of Jesus Christ and keep records well, then an accumulation of continuing personal revelation that consistently pans out brings with it a growing conviction with time, and an abiding inner peace. Our personal journals are loaded with examples of this.

3. Consider also what the New Testament talks about a lot: having faith. Yes, this is something testable: Have faith and act on it, and look at the results in your own life.

All Truth

There's truth, and then there's *Truth*.

An old joke among mathematicians goes like this: "One plus one equals three. (*Pause.*) ...for very large values of one." Anyone who survived (and still remembers) calculus will find this hilarious. Well, at least slightly funny.

The First Amendment of the Constitution of the United States essentially gives us the right to say that 1 + 1 = 3. But saying that doesn't make it true. In fact, a mathematical framework built on that fundamental premise will not safely land a lunar module on the Moon. A famous Abraham Lincoln quote says it even more clearly: "How many legs does a dog have if you call the tail a leg? Four. Calling a tail a leg doesn't make it a leg."

For different but related reasons, worshiping a golden calf (or making a personal god of Darwinian natural selection, or financial derivatives, or the Large Hadron Collider, or political power) will not make everything work for you.

Believe what you want, but if your belief is not based on fundamental truth, it will get you nowhere. It certainly won't buy you happiness – that $20 million yacht derived from your dishonestly earned bonuses and compensation notwithstanding. We are reminded of a Gary Larson cartoon. At the end of a funeral reception, a grand piano, a refrigerator, a television, and a set of golf clubs all fly out the front door of the deceased man's house, and zoom up into the clouds, while his wife wails "*Aaaugh! It's George – he's taking it with him!*"

Arthur R. Bassett (Bassett, 1977) wrote in the Ensign, "One of the facets of the Lord's way of teaching that has continued to fascinate me is his ability to interlace simplicity and profundity. His gospel offers a mental challenge to the most profound scholar and yet has attraction even to a small child. Its doctrines range as wide as the entire human experience, yet *all truth can be circumscribed within the bounds of a few simple, central principles*" (emphasis added).

Don Lind, the Church of Jesus Christ astronaut, earned a PhD in high-energy physics from the University of California, Berkeley (also our alma mater). After retirement from NASA, he also served as a member of the Portland, Oregon, Temple presidency from 1995 to 1998. Don once gave a lecture which we attended at the University of Arizona. During his talk he made several statements that have stuck with us ever since, including the following (Lind, 1973):

> "This is the only religion that I can adhere to and not have to believe one thing on Sunday and another thing the other six days of the week."

His point here was this: there is no incompatibility between my faith and my science. They are not mutually exclusive. Implicit in this is also his clear understanding of the Church of Jesus Christ of Latter-Day Saints 9th Article of Faith:

> "We believe all that God has revealed, all that He does now reveal, and we believe that He will yet reveal many great and important things pertaining to the Kingdom of God."

Our point here is this: science and religion are different means for reaching the same end – the Truth with a capital "T" – and science and religion are definitely converging.

Cosmology and Hymns

A surprising convergence of science and religion

We are both scientists, and as such we carefully and sometimes rather tediously gather and analyze data on a wide range of topics, then home in on a number of different kinds of truth, and then publish it in a book or scientific journal.

We're also members of the Church of Jesus Christ. The Church's doctrine we subscribe to is found in surprisingly many sources, both ancient and modern, including the Standard Works, Statements of the First Presidency, General Conference talks... and even Hymns. At least two very interesting, uniquely Church of Jesus Christ doctrinal concepts are found ONLY in the "LDS Church Hymn Book." For example, here are two stanzas from Hymn #284:

> 1. If you could hie to Kolob
> In the twinkling of an eye,
> And then continue onward
> With that same speed to fly,
> Do you think that you could ever,
> Through all eternity,
> Find out the generation
> Where Gods began to be?
>
> 2. Or see the grand beginning,
> Where space did not extend?
> Or view the last creation,
> Where Gods and matter end?
> Methinks the Spirit whispers,
> "No man has found 'pure space,'
> Nor seen the outside curtains,
> Where nothing has a place."

That's a fair description, if you avoid modern physics terminology, of what cosmologists have learned in the past half century about the universe. Kolob (see the chapter titled "Sgr-A* and Kolob") appears to be close to the center of the galaxy. No "pure space"? He's right – because we now know there is vacuum energy no matter how empty the "space."

Electrons and positrons constantly pop out of nowhere. And there's "dark energy" besides that (also discussed in a later chapter).

And where ARE the "outside curtains," the bounds of the universe? Current cosmology, just calculating from proto-galaxies that we can see *now* from 13 billion years ago, suggests the radius to the Outer Edge must be *at least* 40 billion light-years (Gott et al., 2005).

How about "See the grand beginning, where space did not extend"? To us, this clearly refers to the microseconds after the Big Bang, as a singularity began to unfold and fill space. For 300,000 years light couldn't get out of the dense seething plasma because electrons and nuclei hadn't formed yet. The details of this epoch are poorly understood, and even then, only by using plasma experiments and mathematical modeling. These things were not even known in the 1960's and 1970's. Keep in mind that mathematical modeling of the Big Bang, and String Theory, are very different things. The former back-calculates conditions from observable data, whereas the latter is a theory of everything that unfortunately has 10^{500} possible solutions that you cannot really constrain – it can predict anything you want.

However, William Wines Phelps wrote this hymn nearly *two centuries ago*. The first time we sang it, we liked the music but the words didn't make a lot of sense. Later we earned advanced degrees, and a childhood interest in stars and galaxies gave way to a research interest in astrophysics and cosmology.

There is an interesting side implication of the last stanza, which we correlate with vacuum energy. If the sudden appearance of paired particles occurs next to the event horizon of a black hole (the "point of no return" for light and anything else that falls in), one particle will fall into the black hole and one will not. This means, among other things, that Black Holes are "gray and fuzzy," and that without additional matter drawn in will fade with time (although extremely slowly), and the information that passes the event horizon may *not*, in fact, be lost (Hawking, 2001). Stephen Hawking and Roger Penrose, two of the greatest theoretical physicists alive, had a long-standing bet on this. (Penrose won the case of beer when Hawking finally conceded the point; there is no direct physical proof for ANY of this, or course.)

While theoretical particle physics has focused on String Theory for nearly 40 years, there have been huge advances in biology and cosmology during that time. Recent advances in cosmology have included an improved understanding of the Big Bang – how matter and energy expanded (in incomprehensible violence where the laws of physics may have been different) from a single point in empty space. Or perhaps space itself didn't exist beforehand. Some additional understandings have implications for the speed of light limitation. *Quantum entanglement* appears to prove that information can be transmitted faster than the speed of light. Vacuum energy implies that there is an underlying energy field in what might appear to be empty space.

We rediscovered W.W. Phelps' hymn a few years ago and were stunned. We read it several times to make sure we understood the implications. Phelps died in 1872, and during his lifetime he did NOT have access to *Nature*, *Discovery*, or *Phys. Rev. Letters* – but he *did* have another source of information: direct personal revelation – a way that individuals can receive information directly from God, unmediated by religious authorities. That sure soaks some preachers' business models! This is a doctrine that most people on the planet instinctively understand and believe, but it is NOT preached by any other religion that we are aware of. In fact, it draws the vociferous ire of a number of fundamentalist Christians and Muslims.

This hymn, for us, is yet another tangible and reassuring piece of evidence that all truth comes from, and leads to, a single source. Phelps was interested in something, thought and prayed about it, and quietly penned words to a hymn with content that cosmologists and astrophysicists finally figured out with several billion dollars' worth of instrumentation – a century and a half later.

Spirit Is Matter

Just a different, much more ubiquitous kind

From the Church of Jesus Christ of Latter-day Saints' (the preferred name; it's commonly called the Mormon Church) modern scripture, the Doctrine & Covenants, Section 131:

> 7 There is no such thing as immaterial matter. All spirit is matter, but it is more fine or pure, and can only be discerned by purer eyes;
>
> 8 We cannot see it; but when our bodies are purified we shall see that it is all matter.

Until a few decades ago, this statement was confusing to some Church members and drew ridicule from some non-members. However, during the latter part of the 20th century astronomers had noticed, using red shifts (moving-away form of Doppler shifts of starlight) and point-mass counts, that galaxies were spinning far faster than could be explained by the visible matter in them. This wasn't a small amount of disparity, either: in some cases, the galactic spin was an order of magnitude too fast for the galaxy to hold together. Speculation first turned to invisible gas, or dust, but scans on bands from infra-red to X-Ray showed that these together couldn't account for anywhere near what was observed: spiral arms of galaxies were rotating so fast that they should be flinging themselves out into intergalactic space. The only feasible explanation was that there was additional matter in the galaxies, increasing the pull of gravity sufficiently to hold the galaxies together. We're talking 5 to 6 times more "dark matter," as it was dubbed, than visible matter.

In the last decade of the 20th century, the newer and bigger telescopes coming online were able to reach farther and farther back into deep time: to see light emitted almost back to the time of the Big Bang, calculated from various different means to be about 13.8 billion years ago. One can use several different kinds of "Standard Candle" (cosmic distance-measuring methods) to figure how far away a given galaxy is. A problem popped up as they reached farther and farther back in time, however. Remember that light, though extremely fast, takes a finite amount of time to travel a given distance. Thus, the greater the red shift, the faster the object is moving away, which means it's a greater distance away, and also means it was that much longer ago that the object separated from what became our galaxy. We already knew about visible or baryonic matter, and now we knew that dark matter was out there also.

However, two different groups of experimental physicists, using slightly different approaches, determined that instead of the universe expansion slowing down under the gravitational pull of all that mass, the expansion of the universe is actually *accelerating*. In other words, the universe is expanding faster with time (Perlmutter, et al., 1997; Riess et al., 1998). This won the Nobel Prize for Physics in 2011.

It doesn't take very sophisticated physics to actually put a number on this. Keep in mind that one of Einstein's earliest papers (Einstein, 1905) demonstrated the equivalence of matter and energy (this has been subsequently proven in laboratories, solar physics, and atom bombs) with the famous equation $E=Mc^2$. In other words, matter and energy are interchangeable. So what kind of energy field would it require to make this expansion accelerate? It turns out to be about three times more energy than all known visible matter and dark matter combined. This value, now called "dark energy," has checked out repeatedly. The scientists working on the problem, despite pressure to publish quickly, held off for a long time because they just couldn't believe these numbers.

So where does the count now stand?

Baryonic (visible) matter – the stuff that you can lay your hands on or see: a bit over 4 percent of the universe.

Dark matter (which no one yet understands, but which astronomers can actually measure remotely): about 25 percent of the universe.

That leaves about 71 percent of the universe made up of this newly discovered but still not understood dark energy. One recent close calculation of the ratio of baryonic (tangible) matter to all the dark matter and dark energy for our Milky Way Galaxy is astonishing: this ratio is just 0.0003 – in other words, almost all of the Milky Way is *NOT* "regular" matter. This is a value that catches the breath of any physicist or cosmologist. It means there is a lot out there that we know close to nothing about. As in, at least 96 percent of the universe. (See the later section "Dark Energy – Something Even Bigger" for more on this subject.)

Back to D&C 131: 7-8 – this is a remarkably prescient statement for someone with a 3rd grade education and without a cosmologist's vocabulary. This statement seems to be saying that there is matter out there that cannot be seen by our eyes, and Joseph equates that invisible matter, which physicists have recently concluded forms the vast bulk of the universe, with what he called "spirit." The implication here is not that the latest research in astrophysics proves Joseph Smith to be correct. (Few atheists would be persuaded of this anyway, especially since Joseph equated this non-visible matter with that particular word, spirit.) Rather, the take-away here is that one religion taught back in the 1830s that there was far more to our universe than could be seen. This is now borne out by current physics models of the universe. It is one of the things that make it possible for us to be believing scientists, because there is clearly abundant room in Church theology for scientific thinking.

And vice versa.

What a 3rd Grade Education Can Get You

You've learned by now that a PhD doesn't always correlate with smarts.

Perhaps you've noticed a trend in previous chapters: a certain fascination with what an ill-educated 25-year-old, living 180+ years ago, could tell us about modern cosmology, human health, and the world we live in. This knowledge has interested Church of Jesus Christ of Latter-day Saints scholars since the first years the Church was in existence (Paul, 1992). However, in the last several decades cosmology has exploded (pun intended) into a broader understanding that appears to us to more and more closely mirror what Joseph Smith began teaching in the 1830's. We will spend much of this book reviewing these new discoveries. Of particularly interest to us are the implications of the extraordinarily tiny ratio of biosphere to the rest of the universe. What we can directly sense and measure is just 4% of what we know by indirect means to be out there, and the biosphere is an immensely tiny fraction of *that* (see the following chapters on Candles and Constants, Dark Energy, Biosphere to Universe Ratio – DNA and Poetry, and Intelligence Part III). Even if we count other populated worlds that Joseph Smith was the first to inform us about, where humankind can actually live constitutes an incredibly tiny fraction. Yet Joseph apparently understood many of these things by 1832 (D&C 76: 19-24).

Hugh Nibley published a book (Nibley, 1967) about things that Joseph Smith couldn't possibly have known about, that nevertheless appear in the Book of Mormon and have seen verification since that time in formal scholarship. These elements include things like the "borders nearer the borders" of the Red Sea – tribal borders that are mainly ridges perpendicular to the land-sea boundaries on the western side of the Red Sea that separate different grazing regions; and the name "Sam," the name of one of Nephi's younger brothers. This name was ridiculed in the 19th Century, but the Nag Hammadi documents discovered in the 20th Century in the Nile Valley have shown the name "Sam" to have been in common use among the traders of 600 BC. The Book of Mormon is full of other Semitic cultural artifacts, too, including those unusual phrase constructions (e.g., "And it came to pass," "I dreamed a dream," and so on; see Stubbs, 2016). John Welsh (Welsh, 1961, 1987) discovered chiasmus, a mirror-repeat literary structure common in Hebrew which does not survive translation into modern Bibles – yet is found all through the Book of Mormon. There are hundreds and hundreds of examples like this.

We have some personal experiences that we could add to that huge and still-growing *Since Cumorah* list. Between us we have traveled along about 70 percent of the Lehite Trail in the Arabian Peninsula, and one of us served as chief scientist for volcano hazards in the US Geological Survey and helped monitor the 1980 eruption of Mount St Helens. In the next few chapters, we will be providing abbreviated outlines of some of these experiences, and how they both connect to things described in the Book of Mormon – things that a farm boy in 1828 could never have known. Joseph Smith dictated the content of the Book of Mormon in about 53 days. At the time he had approximately 3.5 years of formal elementary school education.

It's remarkable what you can do with just a 3rd grade education.

How to Deal With a Corpse in Hot Weather

Something as valuable as gold... For quite a long time, in fact

How DO you deal with a corpse when it's sweltering?

The short answer, used by our poorer ancestors, was to bury Grandpa. Quickly. Hasidic Law and Islamic Sharia both still mandate burial within 24 hours of death. For our somewhat wealthier ancestors, the answer was to use deodorant on Grandpa – and *then* bury him when more convenient. For our really wealthy ancestors, it was to use deodorant, remove and can the internal organs, paint what's left with pitch, let Grandpa dry out, and build a huge mausoleum around him... a pyramid would be even better (it's slightly harder for thieves to break into).

The preferred pre-burial deodorant du jour from well before 600 BC until the Middle Ages is golden brown in color. It's still used in Catholic and Orthodox Christian funerals in fragrant-smoke-distribution devices called censers. These are generally brass containers dangled from a chain, with a piece of charcoal in the bottom and a crystal or two of the aromatic spice on top of the burning coal. This golden crystalline stuff is found as sap leaking out of knife-slashes in the bark of an unassuming bush found mainly in the Omani mountains. It's called frankincense. It is wonderfully fragrant. A tiny nugget of frankincense, with some raisins and cashews, will do wonders for a huge bowl of basmati rice.

A careful reading of 1 Nephi 1 through 1 Nephi 17 in the Book of Mormon comes across to a modern archeologist or geographer as a startlingly accurate description of the Frankincense Trail – the biggest trade route of antiquity, predating the Asiatic Silk Road. Scholars in the 1990's found a small tribe on the northwestern Yemeni coast whose name is, using the standard three consonants for an Arabic word: م ﺣ ﻥ . In reverse (western) character order, this is *NHM*. This could be pronounced 'naheem" "nuhom", "niham" – or *Nahom*, depending on where the diacritical marks are added, something first introduced in the 9th to 11th centuries AD, long after the original Qu'ran was compiled, and a much longer time since the Lehites existed in Arabia. The land any tribe occupies is traditionally named after that tribe; thus, Americans are the "tribe" occupying America, French occupy France, the English occupy England, and so on.

Think: *make a left turn at Nahom.* See 1 Ne 16:34: *"And it came to pass that Ishmael died, and was buried in the place which was called Nahom."*

Cities along the Frankincense trade route from Jerusalem to the Nile Valley, and from Jerusalem to the southern Arabian Peninsula, were frequently Jewish cities. With one notable exception, that city ownership tidbit was figured out only in the past century. When Muhammad, the founder of Islam, first arrived in Madinah around 632 AD, he encountered two warring Jewish tribes – or what we might now call trading corporations – and set himself up as a judge and dispassionate arbiter of their conflicts. It worked – and 1.3 billion people today at least read his dialect of Semitic as a result. However, the trading *lingua franca* of 600 BC in the region was not Arabic, but Egyptian – the language of the Nile River Valley, the geographic center of the huge trade network in spices. Egyptian writing by that time had evolved its written form from clumsy and tedious hieroglyphs to a phonetic shorthand called Demotic.

That's a long way around to point you at 1Nephi 1:2. *"Yea, I make a record in the language of my father, which consists of the learning of the Jews and the language of the Egyptians."*

The Frankincense Trail was actually a series of sub-parallel routes mainly predicated on where the oases were – which were themselves controlled by a long scarp, part of the tear-apart fabric of the first of two Red-Sea-opening rifting events. One chain of springs runs close to the coast where the groundwater finally reaches the sea.

Another chain of oases followed the uplifted scarp left over when the Red Sea originally split apart the Arabian-Nubian continental craton 35-30 million years ago. These cliffs rise to nearly 2,000 meters (7,000 feet) high, high enough to trap passing clouds. As the air rises, it cools and drops its moisture, which collects in a line of springs at the base of that scarp – a line hundreds of kilometers long running parallel to the Red Sea. One of those springs is the famous Zamzam Well of Makkah. A devout Muslim wishes to be buried in a shroud dipped in Zamzam water, lying on his left side, with his face towards Makkah.

That's a long way around to point you at 1 Ne 2:5. *"And he came down by the borders near the shore of the Red Sea; and he traveled in the wilderness in the borders which are nearer the Red Sea; and he did travel in the wilderness with his family, which consisted of my mother, Sariah, and my elder brothers, who were Laman, Lemuel, and Sam."*

Incidentally, the borders of a tribe were the ridges between the pasturage for their sheep, goats, and camels. In the Hijaz and Tihamma

Plain along the east side of the Red Sea, there are frequent ridges of lava running out to the sea, some as recent as the previous millennium, triggered by the ongoing second opening of the Red Sea, something that won't be completely opened for another several million years. These ridges serve as grazing boundaries: *"The borders which are nearer the Red Sea."*

The city of Jeddah, Saudi Arabia, where we lived as a family for four years, has several of those springs. The humidity, heat, and salt in the air from the proximal Red Sea were murder on our car – and for that matter on any iron or steel, including steel bows that became available to wealthier traders around 600 to 700 BC...

...and that's a long way around to point you at 1 Ne 16: 13-14. *"And it came to pass that we traveled for the space of four days, nearly a south-southeast direction, and we did pitch our tents again; and we did call the name of the place Shazer. And it came to pass that we did take our bows and our arrows, and go forth into the wilderness to slay food for our families; and after we had slain food for our families we did return again to our families in the wilderness, to the place of Shazer. And we did go forth again in the wilderness, following the same direction, keeping in the most fertile parts of the wilderness, which were in the borders near the Red Sea"*.

As you arrived at the Yemen part of the route, you had a choice of paths: one choice was to go south and then east, and pay a tax that helped sustain the great Sabaean Kingdom (remember the fabulously wealthy Queen of Sheba/Saba who visited King Solomon?). The alternative route was to skip the taxes and take a sharp eastward turn at a place called Nahom. However, you had to risk crossing the desert, where for over 5,000 years bandit tribes have made a living by preying upon spice caravans (Thesiger, 1959). If you took the cheap route, you sure didn't want to light any fires to give your location away – even if you could find enough firewood in the edge of the incredibly desolate Empty Quarter to burn in the first place. You had to eat raw or sun-dried goat meat.

You could still nurse your babies, however (1 Ne 17:2). *"And so great were the blessings of the Lord upon us, that while we did live upon raw meat in the wilderness, our women did give plenty of suck for their children, and were strong, yea, even like unto the men; and they began to bear their journeyings without murmurings."*

Incidentally, the Muslim holy city of Madinah lies along one of these strings of oases. The name Madinah mean "city" in Arabic, so its full name is Madinah al-Munawarrah, or the City of Lights. Madinah in 632 AD was a Jewish trading city – occupied by two rival Jewish tribes. When the Muslim prophet Mohammed was driven out of Makkah, he arrived at Madinah and offered as an outsider to arbitrate between the two feuding sides.

Who do you suppose could make their way through such a dangerous trail, and who could *communicate* with the Jewish sub-tribes or trading corporations controlling the towns around the oases in the trading language of the day? *How about a family of Jewish traders already familiar with the trade system and network? A large family or a small sub-tribe – perhaps with a name like... the Lehites. It turns out that the names Lehites (Lehiyyim) and Nephites (Nefiyyim) are both known from antiquity in south-central Arabia (Stubbs, 2016).* And who could translate the records they carried with them, and wrote as they traveled, in a language long lost to history, more than twelve centuries later, than an inspired prophet?

Because of these and other evidence of the ancient Semitic origin of the Book of Mormon, the First Presidency of the Church of Jesus Christ has approved the following statement:

> *"When a sacred text is translated into another language or rewritten into more familiar language, there are substantial risks that this process may introduce doctrinal errors **or obscure evidence of its ancient origin**. To guard against these risks, the First Presidency and Council of the Twelve give close personal supervision to the translation of scriptures from English into other languages and have not authorized efforts to express the doctrinal content of the Book of Mormon in familiar or modern English". (Church of Jesus Christ of Latter-Day Saints Handbook 2, Administering the Church, p.74), Emphasis ours.*

Volcanoes – and Nephi's Smoking Gun

Evidence you really have to dig into

In 1973 Hugh Nibley gave a lecture at the University of Arizona. We tried to get him to autograph our copy of his book, "Since Cumorah," (Nibley, 1967), but he initially refused. "There are so many better examples now available, some discovered even as this book was being printed, that I'm embarrassed to sign this poor thing." Eventually he signed it, however, and the book is still treasured by our family.

In fact, while "Since Cumorah" was going through the publishing process and for years afterward, hundreds of new geographic and scientific discoveries have been made (and are still being made) supporting the veracity of historical and geographical details in the Book of Mormon. All of these appeared in the 20th and 21st Century, long after the Book of Mormon was first released and were, of course, unknown to any scholar in Joseph Smith's time, let alone a poorly-educated young man living on the edge of a rough frontier.

For example, one item that did not make it into "Since Cumorah" was the surprising similarity of details in 3 Nephi 8 to the events surrounding the 1980 eruption of Mount St Helens, which took place 13 years after "Since Cumorah" was first published. To a professional volcanologist, this chapter accurately describes a cataclysmic volcano-tectonic event on a major subduction zone. Yet volcanoes, earthquakes, subsidence, and allocthons are geological phenomena that don't exist within 3,000 kilometers of western New York State, nor were they known to any Americans in 1828.

Joseph Smith grew up in Vermont and New York State. He received only three years of formal education in his entire lifetime. Western New York is covered with glacial moraines – huge gravel and boulder piles shoved down from their origins in Canada by the glaciers that retreated with the Younger Dryas epoch about 11,700 years ago at the end of the last Ice Age. Cumorah, the hill where Joseph found the golden plates that he translated as the Book of Mormon, is one of these glacial moraines. Joseph Smith had never seen a volcano nor felt an earthquake in his short life. A primitive form of the field of volcanology existed at the time, mainly in Italy around Vesuvius, Etna, and Stromboli volcanoes, but Pompeii and Herculaneum had not yet been seriously excavated. Tectonics as a scientific field would not develop until more than a century later.

Back to Mount St. Helens: Its 1980 eruption was classified as a VEI 5 event – that stands for "Volcano Explosivity Index Level 5." This VEI scale (Newhall and Self, 1982) is approximately logarithmic: a VEI 4 is about 10 times *smaller* than a VEI 5 event, and a VEI 6 is about 10 times *greater* than MSH 1980. Third Nephi, chapter 8, describes a geological event that would rank somewhere between a VEI 6 and a VEI 7. In 3 Nephi 8 we encounter expressions such as *"...there were exceedingly sharp lightnings...",* *"...the city of Moroni did sink into the depths of the sea...", "...the whole face of the land was changed...", "...there was darkness upon the face of the land...",* and *"...the inhabitants thereof who had not fallen could feel the vapor of darkness..."* describing the disaster that engulfed the Nephites nearly 2,000 years ago.

Huge, hot pyroclastic density currents and tephra typically burn and bury all living things within their reach during these events, and completely reshape the face of the land. Magnitude 8+ earthquakes sink cities and everything else – there is a drowned forest in Puget Sound that was sunk by the January 1700 AD subduction megathrust earthquake (Atwater and others, 2005; 2015). Earthquakes this violent commonly redistribute whole sections of mountains to cover and fill valleys, sometimes even causing flanks of mountains to slide so fast that they fly through the air before they hit; these are called allocthons by geologists; and these monster events make smooth places very, very rough. The relatively small (by comparison) eruption of Mount St Helens in 1980 created the largest landslide in *recorded human history.*

For "vapor of darkness" substitute "volcanic ash" and everything falls precisely into place. This kind of ash suffocated many of the people who died during the eruption of Mount St Helens on May 18, 1980; and the city of Yakima, Washington, was essentially shut down hours later as a meter-thick blanket of ash fell on the town. Contemporary descriptions and video tell us that day turned to night and the street lights came on around noon (Waitt, 2015). It is important to keep in mind that the May 18, 1980 eruption of Mount St Helens was relatively small when compared to ash and tephra falls now well documented in Central America.

Central America, of course, is an integral part of the Pacific Ring of Fire, so called because of the string of volcanoes that all lie just inland from the Pacific Ocean margins. The Ring of Fire includes hundreds of volcanoes, some of them HUGE, including supervolcanoes like Cerro Hudson in southern Chile, Masaya in Nicaragua, Katmai and Veniaminof, in the Aleutians, Sheveluch and the Mutnovski-Gorely complex in Kamchatka,

Aira in Japan, and Taupo in New Zealand. We can't leave out Mount Pinatubo in the Philippines, whose 1992 eruption lowered the worldwide temperature by two degrees Celsius, and we must include the long arc of volcanoes in Indonesia fronting the Indian Oceanic plate, including the monster Toba. The phenomenal eruption of the Toba supervolcano around 72,000 years ago may have reduced the proto-human population on Earth to less than 10,000 individuals, according to genetic studies (Gibbons, 1993; Ambrose, 1998).

All these volcanoes (except the Indonesian archipelago volcanoes like Toba) lie just inland of the Pacific Ocean margins because they lie just above their sources: the down-going Pacific Ocean seafloor that is being over-ridden by continental margins all around it. Linking each over-riding continental plate with its subducting oceanic plate are huge subduction faults. These subducting plates are the sources of the largest earthquakes in Earth's recorded history, including the magnitude 9.5 Valdivia earthquake of 1960 in Chile (which caused a tsunami that destroyed downtown Hilo, Hawai'i, about 8 hours later). Other subduction earthquakes include the magnitude 8.7 to 9.2 Cascadia event of 1700, which sank an entire forest in Puget Sound, and then created the "Orphan Tsunami" that destroyed villages on the Japanese east coast (Atwater and others, 2005; 2015). The magnitude 8.6 Aceh subduction earthquake of 2004 triggered a tsunami that killed over 250,000 people along the Indian Ocean margins. The magnitude 9.0 Tohoku Earthquake of 2011 triggered the meltdown of the Fukushima-Di-Ichi nuclear plant and devastated the northeastern Japanese coast yet again.

During the colonization of Central and South America by Spain, a number of regional Central American capitals (including Santiago de Guatemala, and Managua, Nicaragua) were *repeatedly* buried and/or pulverized. In each case, the city had to be entirely rebuilt, often in a different location. To say that earthquakes and related volcanic tephra-falls have changed the face of the land in Central America would be an understatement.

Since the 1963 eruption that created the island of Surtsey, Iceland, and especially since the 1980 eruption of Mount St Helens, volcanologists have known that lightning storms are closely associated with Plinian eruptions (named for Pliny the Elder, killed by the eruption of Vesuvius in 79 AD). This is because of the prodigious electric charge dragged aloft along with the vast amounts of volcanic ash that are blasted up to the stratosphere. Those electric charges accumulate until voltage differences are so great that they must discharge back to the earth via lightning.

But what caused the "vapor of darkness" described in 3 Nephi 19 and 20? This was almost certainly a smothering blanket of volcanic ash. As attention-garnering as it was, Mount St. Helens 1980 was a relatively small eruption (as we said earlier, a "mere" VEI level 5). Yet this event still lofted about 3 cubic kilometers of material and left nearly a meter-thick blanket of ash on Yakima, Washington, 240 kilometers to the east, within a few hours of its eruption (Waitt, 2015). Can ash put out fires? Yes – ask any forest fire fighter (one of us worked his way through college fighting forest fires each summer) or ask anyone who learned how to shovel dirt and ashes onto a campfire to smother it.

So, what caused all this destruction? To get a handle on a "smoking gun" responsible for 3 Nephi 8, we must examine the largest volcanic eruptions in Central America (Sigurdsson et al., 2000; Jordan, 2003; Kutterolf, et al. 2008; Grover, 2014). One sneaky but efficient way to do this is to accumulate information on *tephra*, the fragmental (pea-to-cantaloupe-size) material blown out by a volcanic eruption. More to the point, we want to know how *far* the tephra reached (we are not really interested in ash here, because ash can travel all around the world). The greater the distance that the tephra falls reached, the larger the eruption. Two events stand out:

- Masaya volcano, Nicaragua, about 2,100 +/- 100 years ago. It deposited tephra as far as 170 km distant.
- Chiletepe volcano, Nicaragua, erupted about 1,900 +/- 100 years ago and dropped tephra as far as 570 km distant.
  Note that these dates are approximate (see Kutterolf, et al., 2008).

The Masaya eruption lofted approximately 8 cubic kilometers of ash and tephra, nearly three times more than Mount St Helens in 1980. Both Chiletepe and Masaya lie east of the subduction zone where the Cocos Plate is being over-ridden by the Caribbean Plate at a rate of nearly 7 cm/year.

This rate of crustal movement is important, because it is nearly three times faster than the Cascadia subduction rate in the Pacific Northwest of the US. This faster subduction rate means that there are proportionally larger and more frequent volcanic eruptions in Nicaragua than in the Washington and Oregon Cascades. Central America is basically a gargantuan pile of volcanic lava, tephra, and ash covered with recent soils and vegetation. In that sense, 3 Nephi 8 doesn't record a particularly remarkable event for Central America – except for the timing of it.

In other words, the Book of Mormon is *fully conformable with the geologic record of Central America.*

This subduction-earthquake-volcano cataclysm is just one example among many where modern science seems to be converging with events and geographical details recounted in the Book of Mormon. Other examples include linguistics (for instance chiasmus, Egyptian names, and other Semitic cognates seen in the Bible (see Welsh, 1969; 1981), and the remarkable correlations of the first 17 chapters of the Book of Mormon with the still-accumulating details of the Frankincense Trail (see Hilton and Hilton, 1976; Givens, 2002). The stories recorded in the Book of Mormon by prophets over the 1,021 years of its internal history are remarkably consistent with geologic, geographical, and historical evidence now known. The Uto-Aztecan language group in the Western Hemisphere is loaded with both cognates and fossil linguistic structures *only found in Semitic languages of the Arabian Peninsula* (Stubbs, 2016).

None of this information, however, was available in Joseph Smith's lifetime. None of it "proves" the veracity of the Book of Mormon, but it is certainly part of a rapidly-growing, startling – and rather compelling – series of hints at that direction.

Dinosaurs and Humans. Wait. *HUMANS*?!??

Navigating between truth, *Truth*, and garbage in a post-truth world

Note: To make a point here, all the references for this chapter are taken only from the Internet. Yes, that Internet.

The Oxford Dictionary word for 2016 was "Post-Truth." That really rings a bell with us. We are both persistently astounded at seeing transparently untruthful things on cable TV and the Internet. The word "crap" comes to mind far too often as we watch something on TV that doesn't jive with a previous video, or when we hear about "alternative facts." I'm sure this doesn't surprise most of our readers – that's in part why you picked up this book. We constantly get questions from people who ask us for advice after seeing garbage science or fake news on the Internet; one recent example was how did dinosaurs and humans deal with each other in times past, or variants on that idea. An article in New York magazine titled "*How Much of the Internet Is Fake? Turns Out, a Lot of It, Actually.*" (Max Read, New York magazine, Dec. 26, 2018, http://nymag.com/intelligencer/2018/12/how-much-of-the-internet-is-fake.html)... makes it ever more clear how little we can trust the information on the Internet. Keep in mind that there are *MANY* reputable scientists, legal scholars, reporters, federal agencies (including our own US Geological Survey), and others trying to make real (as opposed to alternative) facts available to all of us. However, our own anecdotal experience, strongly supported by Read's article, suggests that there are probably the same number of charlatans, uninformed and self-anointed visionaries, amoral political hacks, Russian trolls, and malevolent know-nothings who are front-loading their garbage onto the internet.

What can any of us do about this problem of sorting trash and falsehoods from truth? The short answer is that *it's not that hard if you think a bit about it.* If we use peer-reviewed and citation-listed scientific literature, we have a pretty good chance to get at the truth, at least for scientific questions. If we ask an actress about the efficacy of child vaccinations, we get what we asked for (remember the old saying "consider the source."). Certainly, we can easily answer questions from people about dinosaurs interacting with humans. In case this issue is new to you, dinosaurs went extinct about 66,000,000 years ago, and the first recognizably human ancestors first appeared about 195,000 years ago (John

Pickrell, 2006, "Timeline – Human Evolution, New Scientist, https://www.newscientist.com/article/dn9989-timeline-human-evolution/).

That wasn't so hard to find, actually. To answer the human-dinosaur question we simply *searched* the Internet – and restricted our reading to articles that came from reputable (e.g., peer-reviewed and citation-indexed) scientific journals. Note that we said "peer-reviewed and citation-indexed" journals. There are so many hucksters in the world trying to get rich without working for it that it probably would also not surprise you to learn that a few so-called academics, mostly in Third-World countries, have found that they can invite beginning young scientists to submit papers to their "journals." Ahem, *for a "modest fee."* There are many young scientists trying desperately to get ahead in their profession, to get a job, or to obtain that coveted faculty tenure. One so-called "academic" in Egypt was reported to have "earned" over $1,000,000 a year by selling publication promises. He simply dumped anything submitted to him on the internet and charged a fee that was NOT modest. He didn't bother to arrange for or arbitrate peer review for any of it. He just collected fees. He has refused to answer questions from real academics and reputable journal editors like *Nature* or *Science* who are investigating him. When discovered, he just creates another slightly-familiar-sounding journal name and starts soliciting again.

You probably would also not be surprised to know that real academics find this kind of practice both abhorrent and immoral. It threatens their own real science! One tack that they have taken to isolate this cancer on science is to use "Beall's List of Predatory Journals and Publishers" (https://beallslist.weebly.com/). It is an amazingly long list of fake science journals that grows every month

How did Beall develop his list? One of us is an associate editor of the scientific journal "Exploration Geophysics" (http://www.publish.csiro.au/eg). It's not hard to do some quick research and ascertain that this journal is citation-indexed – in other words, it is a journal that is rated for how many times its articles are referenced in other scientific work, a key marker for academic esteem and quality (https://en.wikipedia.org/wiki/Science_Citation_Index).

Back to the original question. We rather quickly found that dinosaurs could not possibly have interacted with humans. That's easy, you say – anyone who has taken a science class or two already knew that. But let's turn to the broader world. What about things posted by Russian, American, and Chinese trolls in an attempt to influence and subvert the

American (Ukrainian, British, French, Austrian, Indian, Pakistani, Italian… you fill in your favorite country here) democratic process? How can we figure out what's true, what's *True*, and what is *NOT* true? This takes a bit more effort, but you can still figure it out. To start with the particular question of the influence of Russian trolls in the 2016 American election cycle, we went to The House of Representatives Permanent Select Committee On Intelligence (https://intelligence.house.gov/social-media-content/). Yes, if you have followed the political news, you will recall that there was once a highly partisan divide in that very same Select Committee, with a former Chair attempting to report their investigations directly and secretly to the White House (a major ethical as well as professional violation), and even block subpoenas by the minority congresspeople on that committee for transparent political gain. Nevertheless, the *staff* of the Select Committee quietly put their heads down and just gathered and analyzed all the available data – and in their report (link above) they outline exactly what the "Internet Research Agency (IRA)—the notorious Russian 'troll farm" *actually did*.

Note that we did not go to Breitbart "News" or the Sean Hannity Show to answer this question, nor did we go to the other political extreme, for example Slate or the comedians of the Daily Show. We all might feel safer, dealing with political claims, to look at some of the sources that are more politically neutral, such as MSNBC, CNN, and the Wall Street Journal to get our answers.

Well, you ask, where did we come up with *that* rating? The Pew Research Center, actually (https://guides.lib.umich.edu/c.php?g=637508&p=4462444). The Pew Research Center has existed for generations, and famously guards the integrity of its polls and investigations. The Center is bequest-funded and beholden to no one. There is no "pay to play" here. We thus went to a source that we felt had their own credibility on the line as perceived arbiters of truth. If you are interested, they are also referenced by (trusted by) the University of Michigan (https://guides.lib.umich.edu/c.php?g=637508&p=4462444). Here is their scaling of political reliability of (American, national-level) media:

Figure 1. Perceived ideological placement of media.

All right, but what are we to do about other questions that might arise? Perhaps there are reports about some ordinary person finding the long-lost (you fill in the blank here with anything weird). That feels good because it is by an ordinary person – like me! Perhaps someone else reports that a certain politician (fill in those words with any name) said such-and-such a nasty thing. That feels good because I've already formed an opinion that the politician in question is a terrible person. The problem with the Internet is that it tends to feed our confirmation bias. That means that we naturally gravitate to stories that support our personal theories. We tend to accept a fact as real data, when it turns out to be just a single point of data, and not representative of the larger world out there – it is not *evidence*.

For a quick training session on navigating our modern "post-truth" world, check out this video: Alex Edmans, a finance professor in London, gave a talk at TEDxLondonBusinessSchool titled " ***What to trust in a post-truth world***."
(https://www.ted.com/talks/alex_edmans_what_to_trust_in_a_post_truth_world/transcript?language=en#t-1029117).

This talk includes three critical tips:

Tip #1: Actively seek other viewpoints. Aristotle wrote, "The mark of an educated man is the ability to entertain a thought without necessarily accepting it." Stephen R. Covey wrote, "Listen with the intent to understand, not the intent to reply." And finally, Leo Tolstoy wrote, "The most difficult subjects can be explained to the most slow-witted man if he has not formed any idea of them already. But the simplest thing cannot be made clear to the most intelligent man if he is firmly persuaded that he knows already." Do you only get your news from Comedy Central or Fox News? Then you are part of the problem – because rather little of these are actually news.

Tip #2: Listen to experts. Would you prefer to get teeth-whitening tips from a hairdresser? Vaccination advice from an actress? Or would you instead rather trust peer-reviewed evidence from experts? Think about this: *who would you trust your eye-surgery to?*

Tip #3: Be very, *very* careful with what you share. Don't add to the garbage gyres in the middle of the Pacific Ocean... or in the middle of the Internet.

By virtue of the fact that you, the reader, have gotten this far in our book, we have confidence that with the few examples we have listed here, *you* can find (and undoubtedly have already found) a pretty good approximation of the truth. Remember, as you do so, that we made a distinction early on about levels of truth, and we provided you with two definitions: things that are true, and things that are *True*. That is, the former are things perceived to be correct <u>now</u>, while the latter are things that can withstand the test of time and stand *<u>forever</u>*.

Earthquakes and Weather – What is Linked to What?

Or: Why can't science solve our most critical problems?

To some extent, we can predict weather: a hurricane land-fall up to five days out, a tornado up to two hours out. There are two consequences to this relatively new, science-driven ability: (1) these predictions have gone a long way towards saving human lives, and (2) there has been no discernable change in where people buy their homes and choose to live. What about earthquakes? If we could predict earthquakes, would it dramatically change our lives?

Go back and read the previous two observations.

There are about 60 scientists in the US Geological Survey, including one of us, who volunteer to reply on their own time to questions that come to us via Ask-a-Geologist. This is a place on the USGS website where anyone can ask a question and get an answer from a geoscientist. Almost half the questions are spam. (Surprisingly, many of these seem to be in Portuguese, and, no, we don't understand that either, but we're getting better at filtering them out. About a quarter of the questions are from school children trying to get someone else to do their homework assignment for them. These are pretty obvious, and by policy we are asked not to encourage this.) The rest tend to be really interesting questions from people as young as 3.

Here is an interesting question I received one day; I share it here because I hope my answer will shed light on some of the questions that, from my reading of the daily newspapers, are floating out there:

Question:

"Hello. I was just wondering first if the increased number of earthquakes is a sign of something bigger to come and since the earthquake in Japan knocked our earth off of its axis a few feet is that the reason for the severe weather we have had lately like all the floods in the south and tornados and severe storms?"

My Reply:

The Earth's axial tilt moved about 10 cm during the Tohoku earthquake – that's about 4 inches. It requires some *very* sophisticated GPS equipment and a lot of measurement time to arrive at that tiny amount of offset.

While there is evidence that continents were at hugely different latitudes in ages past (e.g., freshwater aquatic dinosaur fossils discovered in Antarctica; see for instance Smith et al., 2011), a 10-cm tilt-change will not cause any effect that can be sensed by a human being. A long and slow tilt change in the Earth's axis has been documented over time and can be explained by simple orbital mechanics (something called nutation, that you can see in a spinning top), but the operative word here is "slow" – we're talking many thousands of years slow – the precession of the equinoxes takes about 25,770 years to complete a cycle. There is also the added complication that the continental plates have been moving around at the same time.

What fixed point do you reference against? Since we didn't have observers using sextants to track where Polaris was 25,000 years ago, these things are understandably hard to sort out. The pole star 5,000 years ago, when the Egyptians were building the pyramids and aligning them, was Thuban, anyway, and not Polaris (Kallinger, et al., 2005). And 25 million years ago, it would have been Vega.

Let's consider another issue. There is an ongoing discussion within the seismic community about earthquakes triggering other earthquakes. Large earthquakes have been shown to "light up" volcanic areas like Yellowstone and Long Valley with short-term clusters of increased *micro-earthquakes*. Note that italic: these are very small consequences. However, the current scientific consensus, culled from literally petabytes of data (i.e. multiple libraries' worth) collected over the past 50 years, is that distant earthquakes do not have any effect on faults not part of that earthquake's own fault system. In other words, the monster earthquake in Chile during the spring of 2010 did not trigger the huge earthquake in New Zealand later in the fall, and that one didn't trigger the ginormous Tohoku earthquake in March 2011 east of Sendai, Japan. Among other things, there were months separating each event. Also, an earthquake's energy falls off as approximately distance squared, so if YOU didn't feel these, then neither did the other distant subduction faults that broke loose later on. Researchers have studied *syzygy* (Coyle, 2014), the effects of Sun and Moon tides on earthquakes, and have found no statistical correlation.

All THAT said, there *is* a measurable, undeniable, and steady increase in the carbon dioxide content of the Earth's atmosphere in the last several centuries. Carbon dioxide (CO_2) has a measurable greenhouse effect on atmospheric temperatures, and in 2015 CO_2 levels in Earth's atmosphere reached and crossed the 400 ppm level. Methane, however, has far more of a greenhouse effect for the same number of molecules released (it's 37 times more potent, and we're not talking odor here). There are far more cattle now than a century ago because there are far more people feeling they deserve beef steak. Virtually all scientists (except those paid to say otherwise) will readily acknowledge that there is a large anthropogenic component to this increase. This means that humans burning hydrocarbons, destroying forests, raising flatulent cows, etc., are mostly responsible for these increased gases in our atmosphere. How are they so sure? For starts, the levels of ^{14}C are dropping – in other words, the *new* CO_2 entering the atmosphere is coming from *fossil* carbon. Also, if you haven't ridden a horse or milked a cow recently, you might not believe how much methane a grass-chewing critter can produce. Hooo.

It's still being argued – mainly through increasingly sophisticated mathematical models – just how much all this increase in greenhouse gas emissions has actually changed our weather. There are certain undeniable influences on weather (the Solar flux and the great ocean currents like the Gulf Stream, for instance). There are a huge number of variables involved, so one model may disagree with another in detail – but not in gross conclusions. As the cartoon character Pogo famously said, *"We has met the enemy, and he is us."*

You and I may not remember huge hurricanes and tornado clusters from our childhood, but that may just be our imperfect memory. The apparent increase in wild weather events over the past few decades may also be an artifact of how records have become increasingly more detailed and complete over time. Keep in mind that earthquakes – and probably to some extent anomalous weather events – are to varying degrees random things. They don't come on the hour, nor on Friday the 13th, but often have gaps and then appear in clusters – and we remember the most recent cluster best. That's called the Recency Effect or Recency Bias, and is an artifact of the human mind (and why scientists must carefully record their data). Using a statistically more reliable approach – averaging and comparing hurricanes and their strengths for say, the 19th Century against the 20th Century – we are also hamstrung by the fact that there were far fewer recording observers 150 years ago... and correspondingly fewer and sparser records kept then.

Bottom line(s):
- Climate change is here, is human-caused, and it is clearly accelerating.
- Earthquakes are random and essentially not predictable*.
- Neither one affects the other.

However, this is just what science knows today. In 3 Ne 8:6 we find these words:

"And there was also a great and terrible tempest; and there was terrible thunder, insomuch that it did shake the whole earth as if it was about to divide asunder."

This and subsequent verses make it clear that an earthquake and a coincident volcanic cataclysm are being described here. The timing – coincident with the death of Jesus Christ in the eastern hemisphere – implies that earthquakes can in fact be triggered, or at least understood (and thus predicted), *though not yet by modern science.*

To us, this suggests how far science has *NOT* yet gotten in the past century, and just further reinforces the idea that there is more than one path to the truth.

* Recent studies suggest that a cluster of earthquakes on a major fault may increase the immediate likelihood of a significant earthquake *nearby* by a few percent (http://www.latimes.com/local/lanow/la-me-earthquake-probability-20161019-snap-story.html), however this is still controversial in the geoscience world as we write this.

Death From the Sky

Nobody is safe. Ever. Anywhere.

"The Day the Sands Caught Fire" is the title of an article one of us published in Scientific American in 1998 (Wynn and Shoemaker, 1998) about the Wabar asteroid impact event of 1863. This was a Hiroshima-explosion-sized impact in the middle of the remote Empty Quarter of what is now modern Saudi Arabia. As far as we know, no one died and nothing went extinct.

The Chicxulub Event about 65 million years ago, however, wiped out the dinosaurs. (Not all of them died, actually; modern-day birds, tortoises, and alligators, among others, are their direct descendants.) That Chicxulub object (there are still arguments about whether it was an asteroid or a comet) was about 10 km (6 miles) in size. The Wabar object was quite a bit smaller – about the size of a small house. It smacked down in the middle of the driest and hottest desert in the world (the temperature reached 61°C (142°F) one mid-morning while I ran a magnetometer profile over the largest two craters (Wynn, 2002).

While small by comparison with the Chicxulub object, the Wabar object still caused *startling* damage. Geologic and geophysical mapping show that it raised a mushroom cloud to at least the stratosphere; molten glass rained down at least 850 meters (900 yards) away. The object apparently broke up in the lower atmosphere and created at least three craters that we can still see between the moving saif dunes ("saif" is Arabic for "sword," and these dunes are called this because their top edge appears like a giant sharp blade sweeping across the desert). Calculations show that the asteroid (94 percent iron and 4 percent nickel, plus a little copper, cobalt, and iridium) brought with it a kinetic energy equivalent to, or greater than, the Hiroshima atom bomb. The Wabar impact site is similar in all ways to the Sedan and other medium nuclear bomb craters in the Nevada Test Site, save one: there is no residual radiation. There is shocked quartz, there is an asymmetric ejecta field, and there are other minerals that suggest temperatures momentarily reaching over 10,000 C. If you could have seen it happen, it would have been a magnificent sight – but you would likely not have survived the experience.

Here's a crucial point: Wabar happened in 1863. Gene Shoemaker (the father of astrogeology) and I mapped the field site together and we made a bet. We both agreed that the site was very young, *much* younger than the ~6,200-year previous estimate from fission-track dating.

During a raging sandstorm one night we collected sand unexposed to light since the impact on some 1930-era samples collected by Philby (Philby, 1933), from below the impact rim of one of the craters. If the Wabar site was older than a Qur'anic reference to a destroyed city named 'Ubar, then I owed Gene a steak dinner. If it was younger than that, he owed me a Thai coconut sticky-rice dessert, and the dinner too, if he felt like it. Sadly, Gene was killed in a car-wreck 300 km north of Alice Springs in Australia in 1996, before the thermo-luminescence dating results came back. It turns out the impact site was less than 250 years old. Details for the 1863 date are in our Scientific American article (November 1998 issue).

Whew. *A "city buster" hit the Earth 150 years ago?* Imagine that.

Another crucial point: I have partial records that suggest that at least FIVE "city busters" like this hit the Earth (Wynn, 2002a). There were impacts in 1863 (Wabar, Saudi Arabia), 1908 (Tunguska, Russian Siberia), 1930 (Río Curacá, Brazil-Peru border), 1935 (Rupununi, British Guyana), and in 1947 (Sikhote-Alin, Kamchatka, Russian Far East). At least five times in a century these huge kinetic-energy bombs have crashed into the Earth – and that's just on the 29% of it that is on land that we can see evidence for (https://water.usgs.gov/edu/earthhowmuch.html). Fortunately, every one of these fell in very remote areas. I published another article in 2002 (Wynn, 2002b) that showed that these things happen far more frequently than even a radical like Gene Shoemaker had suspected.

Over one-third of the total human population, nearly 2.4 billion people, lives within 100 km (60 miles) of an oceanic coast (https://science.nasa.gov/earth-science/oceanography/living-ocean). The reason? Because the weather is more moderate near an ocean. Remember that at least 71 percent of the Earth's surface is ocean. Something like 20,000+ tons of TNT equivalent detonating under an ocean is a near-perfect tsunami-maker, comparable to tsunamis generated by subduction earthquakes. If the hit centered on your city, it would mean a relatively clean death by comparison to everyone around it.

One final point: *We cannot easily "see" these things coming.* They have to be really big before enough light scatters off them to be picked up by Earth-based telescopes, and you would need many "picks" before you could calculate a reliable orbit. By the time you could actually *see* a Wabar-sized object coming, it would already be over. Since the Earth has substantial gravity, one of these things flying even *close* to the planet will be drawn towards us, gravity being what it is. We can't use radar to spot these things, either. The energy of a radar beam falls off as the distance squared, and even if the beam was 100 percent reflected, the reflected beam would have only the energy reflected, and then that falling off as the *return* distance squared. Mankind doesn't have radar systems with enough energy to do this; if we did, it would fry everything in the sky flying through its beam.

What does this all mean? *It means we are helpless beneath the sky.* It means we do not control our future. You can get fairly good warning of a volcanic eruption, but a supervolcano the size of Yellowstone (United States), Toba (Indonesia), or Veniaminof (Aleutians) going off could still take the few survivors on our world back to the Stone Age. We can get a shorter warning for a hurricane, a really short warning for a tornado, and *just seconds to minutes* warning for a subduction mega-earthquake – or for one of these bombs from the sky.

But you *can* store a year's supply of food and water with the intent to help your family and your neighbors survive a near hit. If you do that for your whole neighborhood, you can reasonably call yourself a Christian – being Christ-like. This is the *real* reason behind why members of the Church of Jesus Christ gather a year's supply of food and water: to be Christ-like and take care of their neighbors, as well as themselves, in case of a disaster.

Slipping & Sliding: How Fast, How Big, How Often?

How much does science really know, anyway?

An issue of EOS, the weekly newspaper of the American Geophysical Union, has a very compact but informative figure in it (Stein and Okal, 2011;

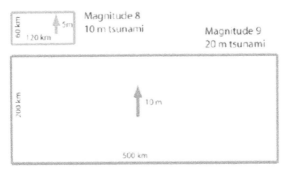

Figure 2. The relation between fault surface that tears and moment magnitude of the ensuing earthquake.

https://agupubs.onlinelibrary.wiley.com/doi/epdf/10.1029/2011EO27000

5). It helps the average science-interested individual figure out how the size of a fault-plane can tell you how big an earthquake will be. Really? Other parts of the figure also warn us of potentially how large a tsunami run-up (the wall of water you will meet at the coast shortly afterwards) might* follow one of these monsters. The follow-on tsunami is what killed most of the ~16,000 people who died in northeast Japan in March 2011. (Elliott, 2014). The tsunami, not the magnitude ~8+ Aceh earthquake, is also what killed about 250,000 people around the borders of the Indian Ocean in December 2004. (Satake and Atwater, 2007).

It's been known for a long time that the *size* of an earthquake correlates fairly well with how much surface area is torn in the formerly "stuck" rocks on a fault surface.

Some quick brittle-rock-vs-plastic-rock basics:

If you have a vertically-oriented fault like the San Andreas, the vertical dimension for the fault "tear" can be only about 10 kilometers – below that depth the rock is so hot and pressurized that it turns plastic and doesn't "break" A magnitude 7.8 event is about as big as it can get for the San Andreas Fault. Even if it rips horizontally for 200 kilometers, it can't get enough surface area torn to have a magnitude bigger than that.

An ocean-floor subduction fault, however, is a different kind of cat. These things dip shallowly, almost flat in some places. You can therefore get a lot more "down-dip" rock breakage or "tear" in that direction with this kind of fault before the down-going slab of oceanic crust gets down to the "plastic" zone.

The Tohoku earthquake off northeast Japan in March 2011 was calculated to have been in the magnitude 9+ range. That's 10 times more energy released than a magnitude 8 event, and close to 25 times more energy than a "piddly" San Andreas 7.8 event (the earthquake that destroyed San Francisco in 1906).

The EOS diagram lays out this surface-slip calculation pair:

A 60 km by 120 km tear, with 5 meters slip along the fault-face, will give you a magnitude 8 event – and a 10-meter tsunami run-up. That's a wave – a wall of water – nearly 35 feet high.

A 200 km by 500 km rip, with 10 meters slip (the Tohoku earthquake), will give you a magnitude 9 event – and a tsunami run-up of up to 20 meters (a 65-foot wave).

This latter explains the monster 15-meter (50-foot) wall of water that hit and destroyed the Fukushima Dai-Ichi nuclear plant, and over-ran and destroyed villages many kilometers inland. This Fukushima nuclear plant debacle now looks more and more like the Chernobyl disaster that depopulated much of the Ukraine in 1986 (where about 135,000 people were permanently evacuated from their homes in a little over a day).

It's been known for a long time that the rate of subduction – how fast a continent is over-riding an oceanic floor – seems to correlate with the frequency of volcanic eruptions inside the continent's edge. Mount St Helens has erupted twice since 1980 (but no other eruptions have occurred elsewhere in the Cascades since 1917's Lassen event). The Juan de Fuca plate "only" moves about 2.5 cm (1 inch) per year towards North America, slow compared to 8 cm per year, which is the rate at which the Kamchatka Peninsula is moving eastward over the Pacific plate.

More plate thus gets subducted down to the mantle, faster, and this means more partial melting takes place, faster. Think of a lava-lamp with three times the heating coils all turned on at once.

What *are* subduction-related volcanoes, anyway? Examples are Mount Rainier on Seattle's skyline, Mount St Helens and Mount Hood near Portland, and Mount Shasta in Northern California: in fact, the whole Cascades range qualifies. Their equivalents elsewhere: Bezymiani, Sheveluch, Alaid and a boatload of other volcanoes in Russia's far east Kamchatka Peninsula; Mt. Fuji and Mt. Unzen in Japan; Mt. Pinatubo in the

Philippines; with Krakatau ("east of Java") and Merapi in Indonesia. There's a reason why the Pacific Rim is called the "Ring of Fire." More pointedly, *all* the volcanoes in Central and South America are subduction-related volcanoes (see the previous chapter, *"Volcanoes and Nephi's Smoking Gun"*).

Does this subduction rate thing also hold for *the frequency for large earthquakes?*

The same diagram in the article suggests that subduction earthquake frequency and size *don't* seem to correlate with how fast the plates are moving. This is probably because of complex fault geometries, and how often so-called "silent" or "slow" earthquakes take place (they tend to quietly redistribute accumulating fault strain and apparently occur frequently beneath the Pacific Cascades).

The bottom line here: the last huge subduction earthquake on the Pacific Northwest coast happened in January 1700 AD (Atwater 2005; 2015). According to seafloor drill cores, at least 7 of these magnitude 8+ events have occurred in the last 3,500 years, but that means nothing in terms of predicting the next monster. *There is no regularity to these things.* The Next Big One could occur tomorrow or 400 years from now.

What can you do about this? If you live in Kansas, you need not worry. Well, maybe you still do – because of tornados.

If you live in Portland or Seattle (or Tennessee, Arkansas, South Carolina, or Missouri), however, it would be a good idea to earthquake-reinforce your house – and buy earthquake insurance. The problem is that if a Cascadia earthquake hits, the damage could be so massive and so far-reaching that it could wipe out many North American insurance companies. Hurricane Andrew (which slammed into south Florida in 1986, the same year as Chernobyl blew up in the Ukraine) caused about $24 billion in damage, and even with the modern practice of spreading risk by underwriting, it stretched some insurance company reserves to their limits.

You CAN, however, steadily build up toward a year's supply of food, and develop some sort of water storage system. Again, this is as much for your neighbors as for yourself. You <u>are</u> your brother's keeper. You could restate it this way: Who would Jesus expect *you* to save? This is yet another way that science can inform our future. If we study, and are thoughtful and Christ-like, we really need not *fear* that future.

* *Depending on fault geometry, there could also possibly be only a small tsunami – for instance a left-lateral or right-lateral fault movement would not raise or lower the seabed significantly, so it would not create a tsunami. Knowing*

the fault geometry ahead of time thus makes a big difference in predicting the size of a possible tsunami, when the first seismic waves at a seafloor earthquake sensor reports back to the Pacific Tsunami Warning Center in Hawai'i and the hypocenter is located.

Superstition vs. Religion

They're the same, right? Actually, no.

Are You Superstitious? Relax, It's Okay!

Here's something funny, in an article called "The Science of Superstition," in the Feb. 16, 2015, issue of *The Atlantic* magazine: A visitor (thought to be Carl Alfred Meier) once asked the Nobel Prize–winning physicist Niels Bohr whether he really believed that the horseshoe he'd hung at his country home was lucky. "Of course not," Bohr said. "But I understand it's lucky whether you believe in it or not." Also find this quote in:

Droke, Maxwell, 1956, The Speaker's Handbook of Humor, Anecdote Number 1172, Title: Not Superstitious, Quote Page 373, Harper & Brothers Publishers, New York.

A Journal of Shipbuilding, Marine Engineering, Dock, Harbours & Shipping, Vol 87, 1956, p. 422

If Bohr couldn't resist magical thinking, can anyone? We're all, always, looking for explanations of things we can't explain. And if the symbolism of the object we're superstitious about fits what we want to believe, like the horseshoe does – a big basket-shaped item that seems able to catch all the good luck in the world, or at least in that room – great symbolism, isn't it! – then it must be lucky.

Because here's the thing: All humans are always looking for meaning, for explanations, for ways to understand and control the world around us. (In this, we're not so different from chickens!)

As Pres. Harold B. Lee said, quoting another religious leader, Rabbi Arthur Hertzberg, about the purpose of religion: *"Man seeks something to end his state of confusion and emptiness..."* ["The Iron Rod," 04 April 1971 address in general conference: https://www.lds.org/ensign/1971/06/the-iron-rod?lang=eng]

Does religion do this? It does. It answers questions that science doesn't even ask, moral questions, where we came from, why we exist, and what we may do to end our confusion and fill our emptiness.

Here's a quote from another religious leader, Shoghi Effendi of the Baha'i faith, about the purpose of religion, from the "Sic et Non" blog maintained by Dr. Daniel Peterson: (Peterson, 2018):

The independent search after truth, unfettered by superstition or tradition; the oneness of the entire human race, the pivotal principle and fundamental doctrine of the Faith; the basic unity of all religions; the condemnation of all forms of prejudice, whether religious, racial, class or national; the harmony which must exist between religion and science; the equality of men and women, the two wings on which the bird of human kind is able to soar; the introduction of compulsory education; the adoption of a universal auxiliary language; the abolition of the extremes of wealth and poverty; the institution of a world tribunal for the adjudication of disputes between nations; the exaltation of work, performed in the spirit of service, to the rank of worship; the glorification of justice as the ruling principle in human society, and of religion as a bulwark for the protection of all peoples and nations; and the establishment of a permanent and universal peace as the supreme goal of all mankind—these stand out as the essential elements.

We're trying to think of which of these purposes, or goals, or functions, of religion can be accomplished by science. Hmmm...none of them.

We're also trying to think of which of these purposes, goals, or functions, of religion can be accomplished by superstitious beliefs. Hmmm... again, none of them.

What does superstition do, then? It provides some temporary relief from the fear of the unknown, a temporary illusion of being in control of our lives. It does not provide any of those admirable principles listed by the Baha'i leader, such as abolishing "the extremes of wealth and poverty," or "the exaltation of work, performed in the spirit of service," or "the glorification of justice as the ruling principle in human society." Or anything useful or uplifting for humanity.

In contrast, here's some of what religion, and faith, can do for us, as expressed by the Church of Jesus Christ of Latter-day Saints prophet Gordon B. Hinckley, in an address given in Oct. 1981(https://www.lds.org/general-conference/1981/10/faith-the-essence-of-true-religion?lang=eng). Speaking of his experiences as an apostle, he said:

"...these have been challenging years, filled with worrisome responsibility and satisfying experience. Mine has been the opportunity to meet with the Saints over the world. I have been in your homes in many parts of the earth, and I wish to thank you for your kindness and hospitality. I have been in your meetings and listened to your declarations of faith and your expressions of testimony. I have wept with some in your sorrow and rejoiced with many in your accomplishments. My faith has grown, my knowledge has broadened, my love for our Father's children has strengthened wherever I have gone."

In what way is this at all like superstition? In no way at all. True religion, then, as opposed to superstition, is uplifting and inspiring, and leads humans to treat each other better, to increase in love and understanding of each other, and to grow in faith.

In religious documents such as the Old and New Testaments, a sharp line is drawn between superstition and true religion.

There are, from the Old Testament, the stories of Moses confounding the Pharaoh's sorcerers. Remember when Moses threw his staff on the ground, and it turned into a serpent (Exodus 7:10)? Remember how then the sorcerers threw their staffs on the ground, and they also became serpents? And then Moses's serpent ate all of theirs (Exodus 7:12)? Remember how much that impressed the Pharaoh and his sorcerers? (*Not at all*: See Exodus 7:13.) And so on.

For instance, here's a modern retelling of the story of the Prophet Elijah confounding the priests of Baal from the Chabad.org website: https://www.chabad.org/library/article_cdo/aid/3942331/jewish/The-Story-of-Elijah-and-the-Prophets-of-Baal-on-Mount-Carmel.htm. You can re-read the story for yourself in 1 Kings 18:20-30. The conclusion is great: *"How long are you going to waver between two opinions? If the Lord is God, follow him! But if Baal is God, then follow him!"* (1 Kings 18:21).

Whichever version of these stories you read, you come to the same conclusion: The true God of this Earth and all creation as we understand it, and more, appears to demand our worship. Why? Because he needs our love and respect? Not even remotely. Because WE need HIS love and help.

In the New Testament, we read about Simon Magus, who was so impressed with the gospel of Jesus Christ as preached by Philip that he was baptized. However, he obviously misunderstood how the gospel and the priesthood are organized and practiced: He offered Peter and the other Apostles money for the power he observed in them to heal and give the gift of the Holy Ghost. Peter's response says it all:

> *"But Peter said unto him, 'Thy money perish with thee, because thou hast thought that the gift of God may be purchased with money. Thou hast neither part nor lot in this matter: for thy heart is not right in the sight of God. Repent therefore of this thy wickedness, and pray God, if perhaps the thought of thine heart may be forgiven thee. For I perceive that thou art in the gall of bitterness, and in the bond of iniquity'"* (Acts 8:20-23).

Here's another point about true religion, a point made by Pres. Harold B. Lee in the same speech cited earlier (https://www.lds.org/general-conference/1981/10/faith-the-essence-of-true-religion?lang=eng):

> *"Now, if I may be guided by the Spirit, I should like to talk about another matter. There recently spoke in this city a prominent journalist from the East. I did not hear him, but I read the newspaper reports of his remarks. He is quoted as having said, 'Certitude is the enemy of religion.' The words attributed to him have stirred within me much reflection. Certitude, which I define as complete and total assurance, is not the enemy of religion. It is of its very essence.*
>
> *Certitude is certainty. It is conviction. It is the power of faith that approaches knowledge—yes, that even becomes knowledge. It evokes enthusiasm, and there is no asset comparable to enthusiasm in overcoming opposition, prejudice, and indifference."*

On the other hand, we believe that "certitude" is actually the worst enemy of science. If you are certain, then you don't need to carry out the research – because you already know. It is also one of the reasons for the recurring arrogance of some scientists who seem to believe that there is a contest between science and religion, and persistently ignoring the history of the awkward continuing evolution of science itself. See our following chapter on the massive intellectual fail of "scientism," or worship of science as a kind of religion.

We see this "certitude" displayed in the writings of many anti-theist scientists who seem to have taken upon themselves the task of "proving" that any and all religious beliefs are false, frequently stooping to ad hominem attacks when reason fails them.

There IS this kind of certitude: superstition is NOT religion. Superstition provides a temporary, narrow answer to uncertainty. Religion – true religion – is "...uplifting and inspiring, and leads humans to treat each other better, to increase in love and understanding of each other, and to grow in faith" that there is a larger purpose for humanity. For our existence and beyond.

Finally, by way of summary:

1. Observation is a key. If something makes little sense, you can invoke magic – or the fact that you lack information. There was poor observation. There were bad statistics in a science paper.

2. Keeping a record is a key. We must not be easily misled by a single or limited number of events recorded second or third hand. Oh Remember, remember...

3. Testing is a key. Can your religion survive testing? Can your scientific theory survive testing?

4. Carefully vetting *previous* research – and vetting the opinions of parents and friends – is a key. How did they arrive at their conclusion? We don't have time to always re-invent the wheel, we need to base judgments and research on something reliable – so where do we draw the line at re-evaluating everything?

Ultimately, is it uplifting? Does it lead you forward to be a better person? If you want to know if it is superstition or religion, you can go back two millennia to this: "*By their fruits ye shall know them.*" (Matthew 7:20)

L'Aquila Prophecy

We want *PROPHETS*. And Seers. And Revelators.

On April 6, 2009, a magnitude 6.3 earthquake devastated the small town of L'Aquila in central Italy. It was caused by movement on a northwest-southeast fault in a region long known for tectonic activity and volcanism (there is a reason for Vesuvius and all those Alps). Over 300 people died.

There were a number of fore-shocks, something not unusual for an earthquake-prone region, called fore-shocks only because a big shock followed. These were sufficiently strong that local officials asked for advice from six seismologists and a government official. A week before the main event, these individuals gathered as a panel to review the data, and afterwards at a press conference assured the public that they were in no danger. Their reasoning: that any potential accumulated fault energy was already being dissipated by these small shocks. But then the monster quake hit a week later.

In May 2011, an Italian judge gave the go-ahead for a trial for these individuals. The charge: manslaughter. In 2012 they were all found guilty – and jailed.

What's happening here? Seven individuals were charged in court for *failing to predict correctly* the devastation that was about to happen. They could spend up to 12 years in jail.

Is this right? Can you throw people in jail for failure to prophesy correctly? Italian jurisprudence certainly seems to think so. At last check, the original draconian sentence was thrown out, then reinstated, and then thrown out again by higher courts. *Stay tuned.*

The consequences of this trial are being felt far and wide in the scientific community. There have been impassioned letters sent to the Italian judge by European scientific societies, and many other science entities including the American Geophysical Union.

The US Geological Survey felt sufficiently moved by this decision to host a two-hour-long, web-based briefing for scientists about legal liability for doing their science under United States law.

The bottom line for USGS scientists: if you do your job in good faith, you are not culpable because of several protective federal laws, and you are untouchable by any state or municipal government because of the Supremacy Clause in the US Constitution. That translates to relief for seismologists – sort of.

A volcanic eruption can be fairly well forecast: the timing approximately, but the extent of damage and duration less so. Some eruptions can be predicted five months out; for others there may be as little as 15 minutes warning from the onset of the first unusual rock-breaking seismicity. The short warning usually correlates with the fact that the particular volcano was poorly instrumented, if at all. The geophysicists couldn't see any evidence that anything was up until an eruption was just coming to life, because they didn't have data from close-in instruments.

A hurricane can be forecast in a narrower window of time, but again, the extent of damage can only be estimated ahead of time very imprecisely.

Earthquakes *cannot* be *predicted* (Hough, 2009), though they can be roughly *forecast*. The Dow Jones Industrial average *cannot* be predicted, though amoral people are constantly trying to game the system to gain an unfair information advantage.

In these two cases – earthquakes and the Dow Jones – you can make some statistical forecasts based on past history, but they assume history will be repeated. Most people would consider a statement like *"There is a 31 percent chance that the Hayward Fault in the San Francisco Bay Area will rupture in the next 50 years"*... to be close to useless for them personally. "So, what am I supposed to *do* about it?" But this information is not *totally* useless: you *can* use this number to appeal for more funds to retrofit buildings and strengthen building codes. Or you could also move to the Mid-West and have a go at tornado-dodging.

The *FACT* of your death can be predicted, in the sense that it *will* happen. Forecasting the *TIMING* of your death is less predictable: your lifestyle and parents' longevity weakly correlate with how long you can expect to live, but that's about all that science can say. Statistically, Mormons live longer and also live healthier lives, but a Church friend, a chef, died several years ago of lung cancer from who-knows-what fumes in his restaurant grill.

Scientists are not prophets, nor seers, nor revelators... though these roles are something that we as a society implicitly demand of politicians and leaders. Some of our readers will be surprised to hear that there actually are "prophets, seers, and revelators" around these days. We had these in ancient times, and we have had them again now for nearly two centuries. We personally know people "saved" by having a food storage system in place in obedience to the recommendations of a modern prophet. One of us has lived longer than his maternal grandmother did, in large part because of a set of prophetic instructions he has followed, called the Word of Wisdom, given in 1835.

We all make bargains, in terms of what we will accept as risk in our chosen professions. Field ecology and research geophysics are moderately dangerous fields as a career choice. One of us has nearly been killed by Shigella in the Venezuelan jungle, by a sand cobra in Mauritania, by a hunter taking a "sound shot" at him in the Sierra Nevadas of California, by an incompetent helicopter pilot in Venezuela, and even by the frigid sea in Alaska. As professions, ecology and geophysics are both less dangerous than being a fireman or police officer. One of us once worked as a fireman during three summers while in college, when large-scale forest fires in southern California nearly caught him twice in fast-moving fire-storms. This job is still far less dangerous than working as a Barents Sea crab fisherman, who statistically die in Alaska at truly startling rates. And we wouldn't give up our research jobs easily because they are just so darn much fun. This is the bargain many people have struck with their life: we choose research and learning, but they're balanced with the excitement (and danger) that goes along with them (see the Faust chapter).

As a friend once put it, we make our bed where we choose – but then we must sleep in it, too.

And... Predicting Disaster

Well, then, can you scientists predict *anything*?

An old joke goes like this: "What do tornados and divorce have in common?"

Answer: "Somebody's gonna lose a trailer."

Harold Camping made millions preaching that the world would end on May 21, and then October 21, 2011 (Goffard, 2011). In his words, "May 21st was one of the worst days of my life." We don't feel sorry for him: Would it have been a better day for him if everyone had died? Camping claimed to preach from the Bible, but apparently somehow overlooked Matthew 24:36 *"But of that day and hour knoweth no man, no, not the angels of heaven, but my Father only."*

Here are some disasters can you can *definitely* predict:
- a volcanic eruption,
- a traffic accident in your lifetime, and
- your inevitable death (though not everyone considers this a disaster).

Here are some disasters that you *cannot* predict:
- mega-earthquakes, and
- when the world will end.

In between these extremes there are some that you can "sort of" predict with varying future time-frames:
- a tornado – by a few minutes to an hour,
- the price of oil – up to weeks ahead, and
- if you faithfully and regularly buy Lotto tickets you will have one less car during your lifetime.

Conservative estimates of money spent world-wide to study earthquakes range up to $50 billion – but with no success for all that expenditure. The top earthquake scientists we have talked with tell us that science can't actually predict earthquakes (see previous chapter). We can *forecast the statistical likelihood* of one, but we cannot *predict* one. However, statistical likelihood makes the assumption that the earthquake-generation process is similar to and somehow linked to past events, which is a pretty shaky proposition (pardon the pun) – because then we should be able to predict them in the first place.

Some things are truly random – or at least we cannot find a discernible pattern to them. Roulette comes to mind. However, your ultimate success at roulette is *not* random:

You. Will. Lose. This is because the numbers and payout are rigged against the player.

However, some apparently random events may simply have causal factors still unrecognized or not understood by science. This hope has driven some brilliant people I know to gamble their entire professional science careers on earthquake research, and they have all seen little for it. So far, anyway.

Human beings always look for patterns in everything – it's built into us. If we can see a pattern in something (like earthquake precursors, or bubonic plague and rats), we hope we can predict something (like the next earthquake, or how to NOT get the plague) that might extend our lives. But a number of things we see over our lifetimes just don't make sense, and there is an instinct in us to try to come up with SOMETHING to explain them. Science merely tries to put some rigor into that process: can you replicate it? Can you verify it somehow? Is it random?

When something doesn't make sense, we can either invoke magic, or conclude that we are missing information. There is at least one reason, one causative variable or set of variables, for *everything* that happens, unless we scientists have seriously misunderstood time; the linearity of time is another one of those faith-based assumptions of science, though there is some argument about it stemming from general relativity.

One aspect of this causation issue revolves around the concept of *random*. The reliability and safety of your online credit-card purchases depends on being able to generate a random number. Really: it has to be something that someone else cannot factor, break down, and otherwise use to derive the encryption key.

But here's the fun part: generating a truly random number is impossible.

Mathematicians and computer scientists have spent decades trying to do this – but hardware that can generate a number by a certain process can be duplicated. Mathematicians have gotten really, really good at generating *pseudo-random numbers* – numbers that sure seem to be random. Yet the fact is that the National Security Agency was able to eavesdrop on conversations in Islamabad, supposedly encrypted, on and after May 1, 2011. The NSA knew exactly what Pakistani authorities were saying to each other after Osama bin Laden had been tracked down and killed in their own back yard. That means the encryption keys being used were NOT random. Massive computing power in Fort Meade, Maryland (and a ginormous and not-so-secret server farm in the Utah desert), win again (Wikipedia 2016 Utah data center: https://en.wikipedia.org/wiki/Utah_Data_Center)

However, there are no random events. ***Nothing "just happens."*** The Big Bang didn't just happen. *Something* causes *everything*, and if we don't understand something, it just means we don't understand the principles underlying it – and it's a fool's errand to then just deny that something doesn't exist just because we don't understand it.

But <u>*Someone*</u> *knows all the principles and rules governing this universe.* Wouldn't that *Someone* be nice to have for a friend?

Climate Change

Yep, Nelly, that cow's left the barn.

You can choose not to believe in climate change, but it's pretty much a done deal. A landmark peer-reviewed study (Cook, et al., 2013) surveyed 10,306 scientists, and concluded that over 97 percent of climate scientists agree that global warming is real and largely caused by humans. These are the guys actually gathering the data and doing the scientific analyses – not politicians. No "belief" is really necessary anymore, because evidence like spiking carbon dioxide in the atmosphere, sea-level rise, the disappearance of arctic sea-ice, northward migrations of pests, and decimations of formerly healthy species are all around us. In fact, climate change has been going on since the beginning of time, and there is a huge trove of geologic evidence supporting the fact that our world is always changing. This evidence comes from stable isotopes in lake sediments. It comes from fossil evidence such as cold-blooded fresh water animals whose remains have been found in Antarctica. It comes from packrat middens (ancient packrat nests that can be dated using ^{14}C) and tree-rings (Thompson, 1990). One of us has visited Anasazi building sites in the southwestern United States, and the density of these structures in now-waterless lands prove that a large number of people lived in a region that today could no longer support even a fraction of that evident population. We could fill our house with all the documentary evidence that has been accumulating that shows our climate has changed and is changing.

What climate-change deniers are hollering most about these days is a slightly more specific question: how much of the recent climate change is anthropogenic – that is, caused by humans? It's no surprise to anyone that we are using more fossil fuels today than are being replenished, by many orders of magnitude. Records kept since the 1950's at an atmospheric observatory on Mauna Loa volcano's north flank in Hawai'i show a steady rise in CO_2 in our atmosphere, from 312 parts per million in 1955 to over 400 ppm today. (See for instance http://www.esrl.noaa.gov/gmd/ccgg/trends/). That's a 25 percent increase of carbon dioxide in the atmosphere in less than our lifetime.

Recently, scientists have made enough measurements to quantify what is contributing to this CO_2 increase in our atmosphere. It's not volcanic eruptions. A USGS scientist named Terry Gerlach (Gerlach, 2011) showing that volcanoes do not contribute most of the CO_2 to our atmosphere. In fact, they contribute a minuscule amount, two orders of magnitude less than the contributions to atmospheric CO_2 from humans. Here are the final measured numbers:

Volcanoes: 0.26 Gigatons of CO_2 per year

Humans: 35 Gigatons of CO_2 per year

And it's *accelerating*: there has been a 550 percent increase in the rate of atmospheric CO_2 emissions just since 1950. CO_2 is a known greenhouse gas, as high-school kids sometimes prove in physics classes. A greenhouse gas is a gas that causes heat to be retained by our atmosphere. Methane is an even more effective heat-retaining greenhouse gas than CO_2 – and the dramatic increase in population in the past century of people who want to eat beef has dramatically raised the methane naturally released by herbivores in their fermentation-digestion process.

How could the CO_2 emission rate ramp up so strongly? Well, for starts, China is bringing one new coal-fired power plant online every week. There are commonly dense-smog days that are declared health hazards by the American embassy, because the Chinese government has blocked publication of the air-quality numbers. India is fast converting itself from a rural agrarian society to a society of middle-class people who ALL want their own car. While some American states and European countries are making small steps, they are nowhere near enough to offset the huge carbon and particulate emissions from just these two countries alone.

There is now even a new name for this era we live in: the Anthropocene. Until recently, geologists broke up prehistory into several categories:

The Precambrian Era ended about 542 million years ago (we start seeing fossils).

The Paleozoic Era ended about 250 million years ago – when 95 percent of all living things died during what is called the Permian Extinction.

The Mesozoic Era (the age of Dinosaurs), which ended about 65 million years ago when a 10-km/6-mile diameter asteroid crashed into what is now the Yucatan Peninsula.

We are now in the Cenozoic Era, which has several sub-sets:

- The Paleocene lasted until 56 million years ago
- The Eocene (when horse ancestors first appeared) lasted until 34 million years ago
- The Oligocene lasted until 23 million years ago
- The Miocene lasted until about 5 million years ago
- The Pliocene lasted until about 1.8 million years ago

- The Pleistocene (Saber-Tooth Cats, Mastodons, etc.) lasted until
   about 11,000 years ago.

Until recently, the last ~11,000 years have been just called the
Holocene. Now the Holocene has been divided up to add a more recent
epoch: the Anthropocene: The Time When Man Started Changing Things. A
singular characteristic: in the last century, mass-extinctions have
accelerated so fast (Kolbert, 2014) that it's comparable to the extinction
event that ended the age of dinosaurs. Instead of a killer asteroid this time,
it's... humankind.

Anthropocene

We have met the enemy, and he is us. −Pogo

Early versions of the syphilis microbe ripped through their human hosts savagely and quickly. Too quickly, in fact − frequently the parasite killed its host and itself in the process, before it could replicate beyond that host. Natural selection being what it is, a "gentler," slower-acting version of syphilis emerged that is now the most common form of this particularly unpleasant STD.

An odd way to start a chapter on geologic ages, you say. But bear with us.

The International Commission on Stratigraphy is the gate-keeper for the definition and dating of the various geologic epochs. This keeps self-absorbed geologists from naming a geologic age after themselves, among other things. The responsibility they have also assures that everyone worldwide is referring to the same thing when they say, for instance "Eocene" (the period ranging from 55.8 to 33.9 million years ago). The Eocene is bracketed on both ends by huge climate change events. This stratigraphic boundary-marking is normally done by looking for a marker bed − some particular earth layer that is seen all over the world which marks some profound change in climate or animal populations.

Here's another example: The end of the Permian Epoch and the start of the Triassic Epoch (251 million years ago) is marked by the greatest of all mass extinctions: about 95 percent of all life forms disappeared from the geologic record. This is called the Permian Extinction (for obvious reasons) and geologists are still trying to figure out what caused it. The lowest (and therefore earliest) layers of the next age, the Jurassic, are eerily devoid of almost all fossils. Then the dinosaurs exploded onto the world stage, becoming increasingly faster, bigger, more elegant, and more efficient (and apparently warm blooded) as the Jurassic made way for the Triassic age and then the Cretaceous.

For the abrupt end of the great Cretaceous Epoch, there actually is a "smoking gun": a huge crater in the northern part of the Yucatan Peninsula of Mexico that marks the asteroid impact that ended the age of the dinosaurs. Think of it: a rock about 10 km (six miles) in diameter made a crater about 170 km to about 300 km in diameter (depending on which scientific paper you read) and scooped debris into a sub-orbital trajectory, (Hildebrand et al. 1992; Frankel, 1999) some of which came down as far away as Montana and the eastern Pacific Ocean. The marker bed for this event is a thin layer of clay that is distinctive worldwide. It is loaded with iridium, a "sidereal element" similar to platinum, but which is not normally found on earth – though commonly found in asteroids. There are also huge tsunami deposits on Haiti and elsewhere in the proto-Caribbean dating from that time.

At the beginning of our new century, a Nobel Laureate chemist named Paul Crutzen suggested the name "Anthropocene" for the Age of Man (Crutzen and Stoermer, 2000; Crutzen, 2002). Yes, it's pseudo-Greek, but most of these things are. This name was intended to spur debate over human influences in the world, and these debates are substantial. What IS the effect of Man? What IS our footprint on this planet?

To put things in perspective:

- We humans are presiding over the largest and most rapid mass extinction of animals in millions, perhaps hundreds of millions, of years. As we write this, more than half of the elephant population present in the year 2000 has disappeared. The last male Northern White Rhino alive (and kept under heavy guard) died mercifully of old age in 2018 (see also Karimi, 2015).

- We are seeing the beginning effects of truly major climate change: a dramatic increase in atmospheric carbon that if left unchecked will acidify the oceans, destroy coral reefs, and begin to drown cities like Miami, Kolkatta, and New York by the middle of this century. It's already drowning the island nation of Kiribati, and Venice, and only vast engineering projects are saving most of the Netherlands.

- There are land features on Earth now that can be discerned from space – human-made features. Some, like city lights, can be seen from the Moon. This is Man's footprint.

Major and abrupt changes to soils worldwide (you can include the mall parking lot acreage in this) might meet the traditional definition of when a geologic boundary is crossed. Well, then, when do you pin the start of the Anthropocene? There is Greenland ice-core evidence for accelerating changes in atmospheric carbon dioxide starting around 1800 AD – when the Industrial Age began to really roar. Then again, there are sudden radio-isotopic changes in soils worldwide dating from 1945, when nuclear weapons began to detonate in the atmosphere.

Which of these dates would you choose for the start of the Age of Man?

Man is now the top predator on the Earth. In fact, with the ice-free Arctic coming on we are killing off even the polar bears, the previous apex predator, the top of the food-chain in the northern hemisphere. To human over-hunting we apparently can lay the extinction of the Mammoths and Mastodons, the North American Camel, the Giant Ground Sloth, and other "charismatic mega-fauna" in North America in the past 15,000 years – just as humans arrived. The eclipse of mega-fauna started in Australia about 40,000 to 50,000 years ago – just when humans first arrived (Kolbert, 2014).

To human over-fishing we also owe the collapse of the world cod population in the 1940's and 1950's, and the imminent collapse, now, of nearly all large fish stocks in the oceans that humanity depends on for protein. A sobering warning – a shot across humanity's bow so to speak – can be found in Jared Diamond's book "Collapse – How Societies Choose to Fail or Succeed" (Diamond, 2005).

In one sense, we could say that humankind "owns" the Earth because of our enormous and highly visible impact on its surface. In sheer volume we are still vastly outnumbered by micro-organisms – but we are changing them also with agriculture and antibiotics. We certainly don't control the earth, however. Virtually all governments now recognize that the uncontrolled and accelerating growth of fossil fuel burning (and, surprisingly, the methane-producing flatulence of the burgeoning meat-animal population on the planet) are already causing terrible changes to our world, including monster droughts, "Frankenstorms" like Hurricanes Sandy, Katrina, Irma, and Maria, continental-scale wildfires in Australia, and drowning coastal cities like Venice. But humanity seems unable to do anything about it (Davenport, 2015).

Which gets us back to the syphilis analogy. If we are an infection that is destroying the earth as we know it, will we "evolve" fast enough politically to keep from poisoning our planet and killing ourselves in the process? Members of the Church of Jesus Christ are somewhat unusual among Christian groups in that we recognize the earth to be a living thing (1 Nephi 19:12; Moses 7:56; D&C 123:7). Since 1835 we have been advised to consume less (methane-producing) meat (Word of Wisdom, D&C 89). Even earlier, in 1834, Joseph Smith instructed the Saints that it wasn't necessary to kill a Mississauga rattlesnake that they had encountered near their tents during the Zion's Camp march (Church History Manual, 2003; see https://www.lds.org/manual/church-history-in-the-fulness-of-times-student-manual/chapter-twelve-zions-camp?lang=eng). These were interesting first steps in environmental awareness, steps predating Rachel Carson's book "Silent Spring" (Carson, 1962) by more than a century. In 1978 a living prophet instructed the Latter-Day Saints not to kill animals for trophies only – only if the meat was needed to feed their families. He also warned that we cannot continue to consider the earth's bounty to be limitless, or to pollute it without thought (Spencer W. Kimball, April 1978 Church of Jesus Christ General Conference, "Fundamental Principles to Ponder and Live").

We were getting instructions more than a century before *Silent Spring* was published. In fact, we have been getting instructions starting with the Old Testament, when Adam and Eve were told to be stewards over the Earth (Genesis 2:15; Moses 3:15; Abraham 5:11).

Have we been listening?

Scientism – Its Fatal Flaw

THINK before you make that bet.

Well, *I* believe in *SCIENCE!*

Heard that before? It's nothing new – it goes back at least to Voltaire.

Scientism is an expression in use for most of the 20th Century and is often used to refer to science applied in excess – or applied unreasonably. The term *scientism* can generally apply in either of three ways:

1. To indicate the improper usage of science or of scientific claims,
2. To refer to a belief that methods of natural science form the only proper elements in any inquiry.
3. To make science into one's religion.

In this third and broader sense, scientism is used to describe the invocation of science as a focus of worship, generally by people who would prefer to describe themselves as atheists. It's sort of like Methodism, or Daoism, or... you can fill in the blanks here.

Two recent articles, "Lies, Damned Lies, and Medical Science" (Freedman, 2010) and "Trouble at the Lab," (Anonymous, 2013) draw some obvious and frightening conclusions about this approach or life view.

They both reference two extraordinary papers published by John Ioannidis, a physician and mathematician, in 2005 (Ioannidis, 2005a, 2005b). These are among the most-cited papers in all of modern science – and they are incredibly embarrassing to scientists. In the first paper, Ioannidis convincingly showed why 80 percent of non-randomized scientific studies turn out to be wrong. Fully 25 percent of supposedly gold-standard (and thus far more expensive) clinical trials give incorrect results. It is from studies like this that the medical doctors that you and I seek help from base their diagnoses and treatment protocols. *Our lives depend on these studies being correct.* Incorrect results include:

- recommendations to use hormone-replacement therapy in post-menopausal women,
- that mammograms and PSA tests are critical for extending lives,
- that anti-depressants such as Prozac, Zoloft, and Paxil can stop depression,
- that doing puzzles will ward off Alzheimer's disease, and
- that drinking lots of water during intense exercise is helpful.

Not one of these turns out to be true. THOUSANDS of stories in magazine articles have been written based on these published studies. Just the propagation of the hoary old "8 glasses of water a day" is astounding. The number of studies that contradict other studies of the same thing are so high that *The Week* magazine actually has a section called "Health Scare of the Week."

Many physicians on their own (including one of our sons), have discovered that just taking a patient off of every drug they are currently taking can improve their health immediately.

The truly glaring problem is that the large majority of these drug-efficacy studies *cannot be replicated*. This means that other groups cannot repeat the same experiments and get the same results. Amgen, an American drug company, tried to replicate 53 landmark studies in basic research on cancer. *They were able to reproduce the results of just 11 percent of these studies* (Begley and Mills, 2012). In a separate study done by Bayer, the German pharmaceutical company, only 25% of published results could be reproduced. These analyses aren't being published by disgruntled scientists, but by editors in the premier of all science journals: *Nature*. Dr. Ioannidis warns that between one third and one half of medical research results have been shown to be untrustworthy. He suggests that physicians, when faced with all this potentially lethal error and confusion... *simply ignore them all!*

Ioannidis' second paper explains why these flawed studies happen and get published in peer-reviewed journals. Without belaboring the details (you can read them yourself if you want to), it comes down to many things – but many things that compound themselves:

- The "publish or perish" ethos for young scientists to get tenure or grants,
- Ignorance of what constitutes statistical significance *among most scientists*,
- Ego,
- Fear of reprisals by peers or superiors,
- The tendency of scientific journals to publish almost exclusively just the "new" and "exciting" discoveries,
- Bias in research study design, bias in analysis, self-serving interpretation, and
- Fraud.

This last issue is interesting, and when identified firmly (often a difficult and expensive thing to do), it is supposed to lead to retractions of published articles. For example, *The Lancet*, a prestigious medical journal based in the UK, retracted an article by (no longer Doctor; his medical license has been revoked) mister Andrew Wakefield that used a mere 12 case studies, performed unscientifically, to "prove" that the MMR vaccine causes autism (Eggertson, 2010). Multiple attempts to replicate this explosive claim all failed, and further follow-up showed that the data had been "doctored" (pun intended), and *basic ethical practices were ignored.*

A University of Edinburgh study of 21 confidential surveys of scientists worldwide (Fanelli, 2009) found that only 2 percent of them admitted to falsifying or fabricating data – but 28 percent said they knew of colleagues who engaged in these practices! If that difference hints to you at a broader problem, then give yourself three stars.

The problem with scientism is that it falls for the oldest mistake in the Book: it worships at the feet of the Golden Calf; one of several modern versions of the Golden Calf is Science. But like all man-made things, science is not something to be worshiped. It is a faith that is based on something that is fatally flawed, because science is very, very human.

Are we advocating that people not trust science? Absolutely not – just don't bet your life on it, and certainly don't pour your faith and belief into it! Science is still far better and more honest than the talking heads and corporate-paid pundits on talk radio or some cable news channels. However, as currently practiced in the majority of cases, science is _not_ Truth, and it is _not_ The Answer we are all looking for.

The Anthropic Principle

A decimal point, followed by 44 zeros, followed by 67

One of the (rather many) unsolved problems of physics is that there are certain constants that cannot be derived from something else; they can only be measured. They just ARE (Barrow and Tipler, 1988). One of these is the fine structure constant, the coupling constant for the electromagnetic interaction between a photon and an electron. Other constants include the speed of light c, vacuum permittivity ε, Planck's constant h, and the gravitational constant G. Depending on who you listen to, there are up to 26 known fundamental (many of them dimensionless) physical constants. Many of these are critical to the current approximation of a Theory of Everything ("ToE"), called the standard model of particle physics. It's not a real TOE, of course, because for nearly a century no one has been able to figure out how to meld gravity with quantum mechanics. The theory du jour (for the past nearly 40 years) for this is actually a mélange called string theory, which requires us to believe that there are 10 (or in some flavors 11) dimensions in our universe, six or seven of them invisible. The main problem with this is not the multiple dimensions (which can't be tested or sensed), but the fact that string theory has over 10 to the 500th power possible solutions. In other words, you can use it to predict anything you want. On several levels it is thus fundamentally untestable, so by definition is not even science.

One must exercise a lot of faith to be an academic physicist these days.

Here's the interesting thing about these otherwise unexplainable constants: if any one of them were just slightly different, no life as we know it could exist in the universe. The only secular explanation for this is the so-called multiverse; we will say more about this later.

One example may be helpful here: the fine-structure constant, which measures the strength of the electromagnetic force that in turn controls how charged elementary particles (such as electrons and photons) interact. This (dimensionless) constant is nearly equal to 1/137. There are several ways to obtain it, but a simple one is this: The constant is equal to the ratio of the velocity of the electron in the hydrogen atom divided by the speed of light. Its value is precisely tuned to allow the formation of commonly observable (baryonic) matter, and thus the emergence of life. Another precisely-tuned number is the strong nuclear force coupling constant. Its value is about 1. A fraction of a percent increase in this value and the strong nuclear force would bind the dineutron and the diproton, and nuclear fusion would have long ago converted all hydrogen in the early universe to helium. Water, organic compounds, and stars, essential for the emergence of life, would never exist. No stars → no supernova → no heavy elements like oxygen, carbon, silica, and iron... → no life.

The amazing, beyond incredible multiple coincidences of precise tuning with all these variables is called the Anthropic Principle. Another way to say this: these finely-tuned physical parameters are a necessity, because living observers wouldn't be able to exist and thus observe the Universe, if these constants were not just precisely what they are. Physicists have no idea why this is the case. It just is.

Even the current age of the universe is critical: if it were a fraction of the current age, there would not have been sufficient time to build the heavier elements (especially carbon, silica, iron, and oxygen) from earlier stellar deaths – novas and supernovas. There would be no rocky worlds with salty seas to harbor life.

Attempts to explain the Anthropic Principle – this precise tuning that permits life to exist – invoke either of two ideas: the existence of multiple universes (the "multiverse"), or an intelligent creator or designer. "Intelligent design" or "ID" is treated with scorn by most scientists because it is un-testable and un-provable, and repeatedly invokes against-physical-laws action by a Designer God, and therefore is even not remotely scientific. In our view, it is also placing very narrow human perceptions and limits on Who and What God is.

But what about the idea of a multiverse? The idea here is that there are an infinite number of universes with different physical parameters – including the ONE that harbors life as we know it – so we exist by a sort of cosmic natural selection. There is also the very non-trivial problem of where all the energy/mass for all these multiple universes would come from in the first place. The devil is in the details, as they say.

But the multiverse, like intelligent design, is completely untestable. Some critics conclude that the Anthropic Principle is more of a philosophical concept, or basic assumption like physical laws, since it thus cannot be a scientific principle. One way some scientists have tried to bypass the controversy is to emphasize the so-called Weak Anthropic Principle, i.e., the conditions that we observe in the universe *must* permit the observer to exist. In mathematics as well as philosophy, the weak form of an argument is one which is easier to support because it makes fewer claims.

It certainly is weak. In fact, if you find all of these arguments either non-explanations or circular reasoning, then put a gold star on your forehead. We personally find it amazing that some scientists are so desperate to avoid acknowledging the existence of a Creator presiding over this universe that they will flail around trying to promote something as untestable as string theory, or a multiverse.

So, who is the believer in something they can't see here?

We agree that there's a lot that science can tell us – we are, after all, both professional scientists. However, we don't think science knows everything by a very long shot. The evolving history of science alone makes this abundantly clear. And that's good, because one of the pleasures of doing science is solving problems and looking forward to new answers. As we show here and elsewhere, there are a lot of ways that scientists must operate on faith, including accepting a lot of untestable assumptions. *Just like believers.*

So, the moral of the story here is you can believe in science and religion at the same time – as long as you don't assume that either of them can currently tell us everything about the universe.

Sgr-A* and Kolob

What's the biggest thing you can't see that is still closest to you?

We can't be the first ones to notice this.

You'll need patience with the following, as it really constitutes a short course in galactic black hole physics. It's not hard to understand – just long. From The Pearl of Great Price, Abraham, Chapter 3:

> 1 *And I, Abraham, had the Urim and Thummim, which the Lord my God had given unto me, in Ur of the Chaldees;*
> 2 *And I saw the stars, that they were very great, and that one of them was nearest unto the throne of God; and there were many great ones which were near unto it;*
> 3 *And the Lord said unto me: These are the governing ones; and the name of the great one is Kolob, because it is near unto me, for I am the Lord thy God: I have set this one to govern all those which belong to the same order as that upon which thou standest.*

For decades, astrophysicists have believed that most if not all galaxies must have black holes at their centers. There is just too much "stuff" floating around, moving *way to fast*, *way* too close to other "stuff" for it not to all merge due to gravity and orbit-decay. They already knew about white dwarfs and neutron stars – that bigger and bigger original stars give way to more and more dense "final states." You can actually "see" one neutron star by its rapidly oscillating magnetic field. It's like a radar beam sweeping over you as the neutron star spins ~1000 times a second. The signal is coherent, which means that the neutron star must be smaller than the distance light can cross in that amount of time – less than 10 kilometers. Calculations show that a teaspoon of neutron star "stuff" would weight tons on Earth – that is, if you could transport and then somehow weigh it.

Hmmm. What happens if you throw in a lot more "stuff" into the mix – what would you get? Must be something denser (see the Newton paragraph below) – and it will be a real glutton for all the smaller stars and gas and dust whizzing around it. Because of tidal and magnetic drag on the highly conductive material, the individual orbits *will* decay. Matter *will* spiral inwards.

Annnnnd... I.... *Gotcha!*

With each cumulative new addition, the neutron star becomes larger and denser, until finally it has curved space so strongly that light can no longer escape it. By definition, it's now a black hole. Matter spiraling into it is trapped.

For almost as much time as they've known about the idea, astronomers have diligently sought proof of a black hole at the center of OUR galaxy. They chose it because it's closer than other galaxies, so it should be easier to image. However, on the face of it this would seem to be a daunting task, as a black hole, by definition, radiates nothing – no mass, no light, no signal can escape its event horizon. Remember from a previous chapter that black holes are really dark gray and fuzzy (but not cuddly). However, there ARE some *indirect* ways that we might see one. As in almost all of science, we figure things like this out only by indirect means (Eisenhauer, et al, 2003) – just as we figure out gospel truths by indirect means.

One way to "see" a black hole indirectly is to map stars close to the galactic core. "Our" black hole actually has a name these days: *Sagittarius A**, pronounced "Sagittarius A-Star" or just abbreviated *Sgr A**. It lies in a corner of a bright region in the center of the Sagittarius Constellation, in the center of our Milky Way. This bright spot was designated "Sagittarius A" by astronomers as the first bright apparent star classified in that constellation centuries ago when they first looked at it. To them, Sagittarius A looked like any other star, but they were using cruder telescopes than the ones you give your kids these days for Christmas. (That nearly worthless toy-store 'scope? Galileo would have drooled over it.) As bigger and better telescopes became available, it turned out Sagittarius A was a whole lot more than a single star.

A very short course in basic orbital physics:

Thanks to Newton, we know that the gravitational force between two masses is equal to a constant (the "G" mentioned in the chapter on the Anthropic Principle) times one mass, times the other mass, all divided by the square of the distance between the geometric centers of the two masses. Whew, that's a mouthful. Perhaps you can understand why physicists really prefer to say things in "equation" instead of in English. A quick translation (I didn't use translate.google.com to do this) gives: $F_{12} = G * M_1 * M_2/r * r$. In shorthand this can be concentrated further to $F=GMm/r^2$. This is important, because a star named "S2" close to the center of Sagittarius A has been tracked since 1992 as it moves in a fast, very tight orbit in the center of our galaxy. (http://www.solstation.com/x-objects/s2.htm). In the vernacular, that sucker is really rippin': it orbits in an ellipse about 5 by 10 light-days across in about 15 years. Days and years here make it seem trivial until you remember the speed of light is 300,000 kilometers (~186,000 miles) *per second.* This star is moving so fast that it makes the huge nearby stars look like icebergs with a dolphin zipping around nearby – if a dolphin could move at the speed of sound. S2 orbits around something that can't be directly seen – but because of that equation above, the unseen mass of "our" Black Hole can be measured, and it's *huge*: about four million Suns' worth of "stuff."

A very short course in basic electromagnetic physics:

If matter is being drawn down into the monster, it will be accelerating because of that 1/r-squared part of the equation: the shorter the distance, the stronger the pull on it, and the faster it goes. In fact, it becomes seething plasma as it falls in, because the calculated forces are truly humongous (try dividing anything by a distance squared that approaches zero – it's like magma expanding and accelerating up a volcano's throat to a spectacular explosion, with ash distributed eight states away, like Mount St Helens in 1980). Such a seething cauldron of accelerating matter will *radiate*: electrons accelerating in a magnetic field give off electromagnetic energy at wavelengths proportional to the radius of curvature of their ever-tightening spiral motion inward. That's a complicated set of words but think instead of a tether ball spiraling into the pole – a good place not to leave your head. The event horizon of a black hole in a busy galactic center, in fact, should be shrieking at all wavelengths. The closer to the event horizon, the stronger the pull and the higher the energy – and the higher the frequencies, all the way up into hard gamma radiation. You need a number followed by lots of zeros to describe the energies involved. It's hard to see the screaming-edge source because of all the stars, gas, dust, and junk in between Sgr-A* and Earth – and it's also a long way away to "look" (about 26,000 light years away) to see anything.

Back to the matter at hand:

Astronomers are a persistent lot, and eventually they figured out that certain longer wavelengths can get past all that dust and junk and be picked up by Earth-based radio-telescopes. (They settled on a rather atypical radio wavelength of 1.3 millimeters – not that far from what your cell-phone uses. They chose this wavelength for several reasons, including because it's *not* a cell-phone-band frequency.) If you can get a rich enough billionaire to pay for it, you can get a big enough array of radio-telescope dishes, spaced far enough apart on the Earth, to get a pretty darn good radial resolution. Think: seeing the shape of a coin located a football stadium distance away. The shrieking edges of Sgr A* can more or less be made out this way. Its diameter is no greater than 44 million kilometers – probably a lot less. This is about one-half the size of Mercury's orbit around our Sun. Now, fit *four million* Suns into that volume – and then step back, or scream as you are gobbled up.

In 2004, astronomers were astounded to find evidence of a much smaller (1,300 Solar masses) invisible object orbiting the 4-million-Solar-mass Sgr-A* – a sort of mini-black hole orbiting the BIG black hole (Ghez, et al, 2005). This object resides in the center of a cluster of seven massive stars, which orbit *it*. Astronomers have also identified a number of additional giant stars that circle around in the near vicinity of Sgr-A* (the "lumbering icebergs").

Now read verses 2 and 3 of the third chapter of Abraham again. Does this ring a bell? Note that this is *not* saying that God resides in, or near, a black hole. However, you would have to agree that there are a number of remarkable coincidences here. There are also some amazing physical processes taking place in the core of our galaxy. Abraham hints rather broadly at a vastly greater understanding than I think most people recognize, and certainly more than a humble shepherd could possibly have known on his own.

Nuclear Winter

"I am become Death, the Destroyer of Worlds" – Robert Openheimer, quoting the Baghavad Gita, upon observing the successful detonation of the Trinity device in New Mexico, 1945.

An issue of the respected science journal *Nature* (Robock, 2011) discusses nuclear winter. Many people may recall that in the 1970's about 70,000 nuclear weapons were pointed at various nations in a condition aptly named at the time Mutually Assured Destruction, or MAD.

Translation: Try to pop me, and I'll obliterate all your cities within 20 minutes.

Atmospheric and nuclear physicists, among a large number of other worried people all over the world, published several papers pointing out that the soot raised by a MAD nuclear exchange would lead to a massive and fatal drop in world temperatures.

Bottom line: those who die in the initial detonations would be the lucky ones. The rest of the human population would slowly freeze and starve to death. As children, this possibility preoccupied both of us a lot.

There is a precedent for this, by the way. About 74,000 years ago Toba (a supervolcano in Indonesia) erupted. According to scientists analyzing genetic diversity, this triggered a freeze that reduced the proto-human population worldwide to as few as 2,000 to 10,000 people, creating a bottleneck in human evolution (Gibbons, 1993; Ambrose, 1998). There are counter-arguments to this scenario, but we don't have space here to jump down that rabbit hole.

Because of these and other studies, Ronald Reagan took steps in parallel with Mikhail Gorbachev of the Soviet Union to reduce the tension in the 1980's – and together they reduced the worldwide arsenal. Today there are about 22,000 nuclear weapons in the world (in various states of readiness or not so ready), and with the New Start Treaty between Russia and the United States this could potentially drop to 5,000. History may not repeat itself, but it sure does rhyme (Mark Twain) and we seem to be on a new cycle of nuclear threats as this is written.

The author of the *Nature* paper points out that there are at least 200 known (if unacknowledged) ballistic nuclear weapons in Israel, a rapidly-growing arsenal in increasingly unstable Pakistan, unknown arsenals in India and China, and a growing nuclear arsenal in increasingly bellicose North Korea. These all pose a growing and very real threat to

84

humanity as a whole. Radioactivity and cancer reach far beyond the destruction zone of the initial blast.

Human history has a consistent and rather bad track record of one charismatic nut causing the deaths of millions of people at a time – Stalin's Collectivization and Hitler's Final Solution at 20,000,000 victims each come to mind. Up to 70,000,000 died during the political convulsions triggered by Mao Tse-tung in China (Schram, 2007).

The *Nature* author, Robock, refers to studies having access to far better atmospheric models than were available just a decade ago. These models can deal with more variables, they have a much finer 3-D modeling grid, and all of the modeling is based on much better experimental data. Here's what the modeling now tells us:

Their initial assumption is a 50-Hiroshima-bomb equivalent nuclear exchange – say, an exchange between Pakistan and India, but Iran-Israel and North Korea vs. the US are other real possibilities. If lobbed at cities, the debris raised by these detonations will amount to a calculated 5 megatons of smoke and toxic soot. Open-air nuclear tests in the 1960's show that this debris will quickly reach the Troposphere, and new models show it will be heated and rise to the Stratosphere, where it will circulate worldwide for years.

There's no safe hidey-hole, either: radioactive debris from an exchange in the Northern Hemisphere will take a while, but it *will* reach and impact the Southern Hemisphere.

Fifty Hiroshima bombs will drop the worldwide average temperature by -0.7 degrees C. This doesn't sound like much, but it is comparable to the temperature drop during the Little Ice Age (1400AD – 1850AD). During this time, millions died of famine in Europe alone.

An even larger exchange is a real possibility – and carries with it proportionally greater consequences. The modeling is not advanced enough yet to even know if the increase will in fact be proportional – it could push the Earth's climate to a tipping-point where a new Glacial Age is precipitated. We know just enough to be scared, and this clearly comes across in the otherwise dry scientific discussion of the *Nature* article.

The underlying problem right now is that the human population is over 7 billion and growing, and it is meta-stable. By meta-stable, we mean that a small perturbation may have huge, disproportionate consequences. There are vast numbers of people living right now on the edge of survival – seeking food on a day-to-day basis. There are already huge and persistent famines underway in North Korea and in much of Africa.

What can YOU do about this? As an individual, not much, beyond gathering at least some fraction of a year's supply of food and water, and helping people in many other ways such as working at homeless shelters and volunteering at soup kitchens. Why would you bother? Because you may be able to help neighbors on your block and in east Africa when (not if) the worldwide food situation worsens.

Taking care of others is a basic responsibility for anyone who calls themselves followers of Christ. It is pounded into our awareness, repeatedly, in the Book of Mormon.

Science and Statistics and Truth

Science isn't the hard part...

What? *Aren't these all the same thing?*

Not necessarily – especially when statistics are involved.

As we've already noted, a weekly news-and-commentary summary magazine called *The Week (https://theweek.com/)*, even has a regular column titled *"Health Scare of the Week."*

Vitamin D cures cancer. Vitamin D statistically minimizes recurrence of certain types of cancer. Those are two very different statements, and the "statistically" part depends heavily on sample-size and sample population. What population was checked? Healthy college students? Aging nursing home residents? Australian lifeguards exposed to the Sun all day? Big difference. Also, measures of statistical significance (T-tests, etc.) must be considered. If you can understand them, that is. More to the point, statistical significance tests are predicated on two fundamental and dangerous assumptions: (1) that the data represent something 100% true, and (2) that one need not understand the relationships between data and reality.

How does one make sense of a statement like *"...found that people with the most Mediterranean diet have up to a 40 percent lower risk of developing Alzheimer's disease."?* (DeWeerdt, 2011)

What could that possibly mean??!? For starts, what constitutes a "Mediterranean diet" anyway? How long do you have to "eat Mediterranean" to be "saved" from Alzheimers?

At the core of these problems is a distinction between Bayesian statistics and Fisherian statistics. For a blunt explanation of the profound difference between the two, the authors recommend Nate Silver's book "The Signal and the Noise" (Silver, 2011). Fisherian statistics is a fading paradigm in much of the science world, but its long-term damage has already been profound. Starting with several flawed basic assumptions, including that no prior knowledge can be incorporated in the calculations, and that all data truly represent only the true world situation, these have led to many of the problems in modern science referred to in previous chapters.

Conflicting scientific papers are a real cause for concern. However, there is no more obvious red flag to these problems than scientific papers with a conflict of interest buried somewhere inside. For an example: one paper (Nemeroff et al., 2001, Am. J. Psychiatry 158, 906-912), cited in the scientific literature more than 250 times since 2001, said that the drug Paxil was a wonder antidepressant with minimal side-effects. However, there have been accusations that the study's academic authors were "hand-picked" by the drug company and *engaged in gross scientific misconduct.* Among other things, they allowed their names to be attached to the original manuscript, which was actually written by an unacknowledged contractor hired by Glaxo-Smith-Klein. That smells like week-old fish to an ethical scientist. The contentious issue of drug-industry influence over medical research is bubbling just under the spill-all-over-the-stove-and-onto-the-floor point as we write this. Honesty and ethics (or the lack thereof), are important parts of this whole issue, and unfortunately the process is money-driven.

And it's not just ethics of scientists and the corporations funding them, but also the powerful driving force that publishers "need" to get readers with catchy headlines for articles designed to appeal to unknowledgeable people.

How can you retain your sanity when faced with conflicting and sometimes even ridiculous scientific and health claims? We recommend the following:

1. Never take something in popular "news" media too seriously – it has usually been written by a so-called "science writer," who may have little actual training in scientific research and interpreting statistics. It's often removed some distance from the original data, and nearly always has an incentive for a sensationalist slant.

2. Never bet too much on a scientific study until there are repeats and duplicate verifications by independent groups. The supposed discovery of cold fusion is an example: When other scientists couldn't replicate the results of University of Utah chemists Pons and Fleishman, it became clear that their "research" and "evidence," though probably not a deliberate hoax, were clumsily done and not carefully evaluatcd. A university fearful of losing lucrative patent and other benefits took their ball and ran away with it, compounding the original error(s) (Voss, 1999; Ackerman, 2006).

3. If something cannot be replicated by independent researchers, *it's probably not true.* However, here is yet another confounding issue: replication studies are *not* often done, because they are expensive,

and don't get promotions and tenure for researchers. We thus have yet another Catch-22.

Progress in science has nevertheless been a growing, living thing. In the early 19th Century, common medicinal practice, for example as documented in the Lewis and Clark expedition (Ambrose, 1997), consisted of giving mercury for syphilis, and bleeding the patient for almost everything else. During childbirth, doctors and midwives regularly bled women into unconsciousness, mainly to relieve their own anxiety at hearing the screams and moans accompanying most births. Medicine at that time generally did more *bad* than good for humanity, or at least for individual humans.

Deduction and experimentation were in their relative infancy, and steps to improve medicine were slow and halting. Louis Pasteur (1822-1895) was observant enough to recognize that milk maids who had been infected with cow pox did NOT contract smallpox, a lethal killer at the time. He developed the first vaccine and then went on to figure out fermentation and the process named for him: pasteurization.   In 1854 John Snow looked at a map of London, and marked houses where people – mostly children – had died of cholera. He saw that deaths clustered around a single community water pump on Broad Street. He arranged for the handle of this pump to be removed, and *voila!* – end of epidemic. Progress, in other words, measured in the lives of children saved (Johnson, 2006).

Perhaps the largest elephant in the room of modern science is the uneven distribution of resources. Is it more useful to society to expend tens of billions of dollars on the Large Hadron Collider to find the Higgs Boson? Or does it make better sense to spend 10% of that money on a malaria vaccine to save the million children who die every year from that hideous disease? This resource allocation issue is always present at all levels in medicine and public health. The media influence this resource allocation process by the attention they pay to some issues but not to others. Do you spend stretched public resources on something like solving tinnitus (the screeching that about 30 percent of adults are hearing every day and every night of their lives), or finding an AIDS vaccine (which affects roughly 0.3 percent of the US population, and rarely kills anymore) – or do you spend your resources on cholera (which kills millions yearly, mostly children)? Which of these options have YOU noticed most in the news?

Doctors depend on medical research, which itself depends on statistics – to correctly compare the efficacy of one drug or treatment to another. The larger the sample size in a research study, the more reliable are your statistics, and therefore your useable results, will be. For example, the results compiled from the 238,000 people being studied in the ongoing *Harvard Nurses Health Study* (http://www.channing.harvard.edu/nhs/) will be more reliable than the results of a study with 45 men taking a drug and 52 men taking a control placebo to evaluate a possible treatment for tinnitus (https://www.ohsu.edu/xd/about/news_events/news/2004/07-30-tinnitus-patients-need-n.cfm). Every additional person in a clinical trial, however, costs the researchers additional money. NSF and NIST grants being limited, sample research populations also necessarily tend to be limited.

We said "tend to be" ... read on.

Keep in mind that there are no black-and-white medical fixes or solutions – not even cigarettes vs. no cigarettes. One of our uncles died of dementia at 96 after chain-smoking for 82 years, while a devout Church member friend who had never smoked died of lung cancer at age 45. This helps us understand another problem of medical research: There are so many variables that it's hard to test for them separately. Thus, for instance, when researchers think they are finding a genetic effect, such as obesity for some forms of diabetes, they may just as likely be finding results influenced by a family's grandparents' eating habits or their current economic status – poor people cannot afford healthy food. Even with tobacco, which is probably as close as we'll ever get to a statistical slam-dunk for a known and avoidable bad outcome, there are always glaring "great uncle" exceptions to the rule.

If you want the largest statistical sample possible, to get the most reliable numbers, ***you have to go to the state level: millions of people.*** Death from all cancers is lowest in the State of Utah (Lyon et al., 1994). It doesn't take a rocket scientist to figure out a correlation here.

Joseph Smith gave that one to us in 1835. It's called the Word of Wisdom, and advises avoidance of tobacco, coffee and tea, and also avoidance of heavy use of meat in our diets except in times of necessity like winter. It also encourages consumption of vegetables, fruit, and grains.

Popper

Philosophy again rears its head.

...as in Sir Karl Popper (1902 – 1994), an Austrian philosopher of science who rejected the traditional idea that science advances by observation, deduction, and proof (Horgan, 1992). Instead, Popper held that knowledge advances through a creative process of developing theories which are filtered out by falsifiability: This means the ability of a theory—a working framework for explaining and predicting natural phenomena—to be disproved by an experiment or observation (Popper, 1959). The principle weakness of this approach is that Popper held that knowledge advancement was an evolutionary process.

Well, Popper was partially correct.

What Popper meant was that the theories that survive are the ones that best help us survive and prosper. When a theory is tested, we consider how it fits with our overall belief system and reject the theory that is most expendable – the one with the least inductive evidence supporting it. This is like cross-pollinating and irradiating your roses over generations to create the black rose that your aesthetic taste has desired. Or think of scholars in the 16th Century, trying to force-fit explanations of the jinking movements of planets in the sky to the Catholic Church's Earth-centric world view. This is not really how science works. Falsifiability is crucial, yes. However, convenience – convolving a theory to conform to our existing belief system – _no_, that's not seeking Truth. That's taking the road most easily traveled.

Thomas Kuhn (1922-1996) argued forcefully that science advances only through a process of observing anomalies that don't fit with existing theories (Kuhn, 1962). These inevitably lead, through a "paradigm shift," to a newer theory. Willard Quine (1908 – 2000) and Pierre Duhem (1861 – 1916) had earlier laid out a weakness of Popper's approach – they were certain that hypotheses can never be falsifiable in isolation. Any scientific theory is really an interdependent set of theories and assumptions, where any anomalous observation can falsify a number of different sub-hypotheses. Falsifiability proceeding this way is closer to how modern science really works (Harding, 1976).

There are also hypotheses that are not falsifiable by definition: the existence of a multiverse, the existence of God, the existence of 11 dimensions, etc. Because these things are not falsifiable – cannot be tested experimentally – string theory and belief in God are not science.

Trying to call them science is why science has developed a (temporary) bad name for itself.

But we must give credit to Karl Popper: because of him, (most) scientists are at least forced to be honest, and we can now more readily throw out "science" that is *not* science.

Theory vs. Experiment – the Importance of Falsifiability

If ya can't test it, it ain't science. Or religion.

For a little more than a century after the great physicists Michael Faraday (1791 – 1867) and James Clerk Maxwell (1831 – 1879), the idea that a theory must be tested to prove it was correct was for all practical purposes a working definition of "physics." By the middle of the last century, the rather attention-grabbing success of atomic bomb development by physicists led to a golden age in physics, with branches expanding out into plasma physics, solid-state physics (where one of us came from), cryophysics, biophysics, geophysics (where one of us is mostly parked now), optical physics, hydrophysics, and astrophysics (one of us has also published papers in the latter two areas), and other experimental sub-specialties of physics.

However, for close to 40 years now, an entire generation of theoretical physicists have been attempting to reconcile general relativity with quantum mechanics and the particle physics zoo's Standard Model – by invoking something called String Theory. String theorists now dominate many large university physics departments, and thus control the hiring of younger new faculty, and you can imagine what this has led to. String theory comes in as many flavors as there are string theorists, but these flavors of the theory all postulate as a common denominator the existence of un-measurable tiny strings – and totally untestable extra dimensions. In an attempt to explain what is generally referred to as the (observed but poorly named) Anthropic Principle discussed above, they appeal to a belief in a totally unverifiable "multiverse." This is an infinite number of parallel universes, of which we belong to the one life-populated universe by a sort of Darwinian natural selection. While mathematically elegant, none of these theories is even remotely grounded in testable reality. Not only is there no experimental proof of any of this, but the theoretical physicists (if pressed) will admit that these theoretical approaches are _unfalsifiable_. That means they can't be tested. They can never be proven. In other words, **_they are no longer "doing physics", but instead are indulging in mathematical philosophy_** (Woit, 2006; Smolin, 2006). The font in the main title of Woit's book is especially pointed: "Not Even Wяong."

It's not science if it's not testable. It's not religion if it's not testable.

The take-away here is that the un-provable and un-falsifiable are not just the domain of the religious. Therefore it's intellectually untenable to attack believers on the grounds that their belief in God can't be proven. Neither can the Multiverse. Neither can String Theory.

Selective Evidence

Why "cherry-picking" has such a bad name.

Out of the blue one morning I received a phone call from a man in Mississippi. Months earlier I had tried hard to answer a question from him, submitted to the USGS "Ask a Geologist" web-link (http://walrus.wr.usgs.gov/ask-a-geologist/). He took my sincere effort to answer his question as sympathy for his cause, tracked me down, and talked long and very loudly over the phone to get me to agree with his theory: that the Great Comet of 1811 was the cause of the 1811–12 New Madrid earthquakes.

Some background:

1. The Comet of 1811 was a real humdinger, visible longer (March 1811 until summer 1812) than any other comet until Hale-Bopp. However, *it came nowhere near the Earth* (Burnham and Levy, 2000).

2. The New Madrid earthquakes took place in the Mississippi valley where Tennessee, Kentucky, Missouri, and Arkansas touch (Johnson and Schweig, 1996). This point is apparently in the center of an ancient failed continental rift, where North America started to split apart (like the Red Sea split apart the Arabian craton into the Arabian Peninsula and Sudan-Egypt). However, the rift then stopped after partially opening up the Mississippi valley (it is thus called a "failed rift" by geologists). The first two New Madrid earthquakes in December 1811 were BIG: estimates from ground evidence (sand-boils, reversal of the Mississippi river, etc.) put them both in the Magnitude 8 range. These are both bigger than the 1906 San Francisco earthquake (M ~ 7.8); and the New Madrid events were felt far more distantly. Two large aftershocks hit the following January and February of 1812. Eye-witness reports indicate that the Mississippi River flowed *backwards* for about an hour, creating and filling Reelfoot Lake in Tennessee, before returning to its normal course (Johnson and Schweig, 1996).

Basic fault physics, and the fact that the Great Comet never came within tens of millions of miles of Earth, would cause anyone who spends five minutes Googling those items above to discard any possible connection.

However, the individual on the phone told me that he had seen a sunken rim near his home, had found "thousands" of meteorites, and even "encased pieces of human bodies" on his property. He also said a USGS seismologist agreed with him but wouldn't return samples he sent her.

That USGS seismologist was someone I happened to know, so I called her – and you probably would not be surprised to hear she had a very different story. The "sunken rim" was an ox-bow of a tributary river to the Mississippi, something common with rivers in flat land. The "meteorites" were fragments of a well-known regional sandstone formation.

I tried to ask this guy how he had dated the individual features to connect them, especially the meteorites and the "encased pieces of human bodies"? He brushed past this and said that I must Google the topic – it would lead me to his website. Oh, right. He had built a website to support this theory of his, *so if it's on the internet it must be true.*

Early takeaway here: treat everything you find on the Internet with caution – even those Wikipedia links you encounter – if it hasn't been vetted with a scientific peer-review process required by all reputable scientific journals. If as a scientist you based your hypothesis and subsequent scientific research on something pulled out of someone's ear, you can bet it won't get you very far – certainly not to the Truth. Not even if you made your own website about it.

As I mentioned earlier, I work for the US Geological Survey, and have specific tasks I am charged with doing. I'm not paid by the US taxpayer to have fun and pursue what I might like to do, so responding to Ask-a-Geologist queries is something I must do on my own time as a volunteer. To stop the high-speed chatter from this man on the phone, I asked him to send me his important points in an email message. He never did... but he called back many more times.

For federal scientists, these sorts of encounters are surprisingly common. There are two common denominators:

1. ***An individual has formed a strong opinion about something*** and is frustrated that no one will agree with him/her. They frequently say things like *"Scientists are set in their ways,"* and *"Scientists won't listen to an average guy if he's not educated."*

2. ***They then do selective evidence-shopping***: if something doesn't support their theory, they discard the evidence. This is also called *"cherry-picking."*

The first issue is understandable. They didn't work 80 hours a week and live below the poverty level for 10 years to get a PhD, and they resent when someone *who did do all that work to earn one* asks inconvenient questions, or perhaps just blows them off. There are issues of kindness and respect here, and we all know brusque and impatient people, whether they have a PhD or not. It's perfectly understandable that someone who is busy on a project will have little patience with someone who didn't do their homework, and says things that make no sense to someone who has studied physics, or astronomy, or geology, or indeed any scientific subject.

The second issue is far more serious: selective evidence-shopping is the very antithesis of honest science. It will never lead you to the truth. Selective evidence-shopping in this case included misrepresenting what another scientist had said; he twisted his encounter with my colleague to serve his ends. Where I come from, that's called lying. A more modern wording is "alternative facts." As you might imagine, neither my seismologist friend nor I wish to ever talk with this individual again, for fear that he will misrepresent what _we_ say to someone _else_ – that he will allege to someone else that _two_ USGS scientists agree with him now. Who wants to hang out with a dishonest person?

It all boils down to integrity: if you're not honest, you will fail as a scientist. It may happen before or after you earn your degree(s), _but you will fail_. When people learn that you have been dishonest, they will never trust you, and won't waste their precious time on you. Sadly, I've known a few people with enough brains to earn a PhD who can't seem to understand this profoundly simple principle. They never seem to understand why their careers dead-end.

Science Requires Honesty. If personal integrity isn't important to you, don't bother to apply for a future in science.

The second takeaway: If science isn't carefully peer reviewed, if it is not consistent with previous studies, you probably can't trust it. This is one way to quickly and easily separate good science from bad science.

THE MOST IMPORTANT takeaway here: The analog for religion is similar: if something isn't consistent with the scriptures, it probably isn't true.

Candles and Constants, and Vast Cosmic Distance

You have no idea how vast. No one really does.

You can sing that to the tune of *"These are a few of my favorite things"* from "The Sound of Music." One of us often does, anyway.

We've got something interesting for you in these next two chapters, probably The Biggest Thing(s) of All. However, getting there requires some more physics background first, so please be patient, because we will simplify it – and make it equation-free.

First, an odd observation: In early cloud chamber experiments physicists would see evidence of paired particles popping into existence out of nothing. They were always particle-anti-particle pairs and they always flew off in opposite directions, so conservation of momentum and charge at least were conserved. But to conserve mass-energy (remember the old Einstein mass-energy equivalence, that energy equals mass times the velocity of light squared), you had to assume that *there was an energy there before the particles appeared.* That energy exists even in a vacuum – and this is where "vacuum energy" got its name. It's real, and it permeates all space. It's been measured in a laboratory via something called the Casimir Effect (Jaffe, 2005).

Another observation: the farther away something is, the more difficult it is to judge that distance. Pluto is not the farthest minor planet from the Sun, but it's a very, very long way away. So far, in fact, that Pluto doesn't move that much in the 6 months it takes for the Earth to move from one side of the Sun to the other. Relatively simple geometry, using the two angles of a triangle and the known distance between the Earth's position at those six-month points, allows for a calculation of the distance to Pluto, and that comes to about 6 *billion* kilometers from the Sun. This angular difference, as you look at something shift as you move from one side of the Sun to the other side, is called *parallax*. Alpha Centauri, the nearest star, is about 4 light-years, or 40 *trillion* kilometers, away from the Sun... about 6,600 times farther away than Pluto. The center of the galaxy is about 25,000 light-years away from the Sun. The Andromeda galaxy is about a hundred times yet farther away. With these huge, multiple compounding jumps in distance, using trigonometry to measure parallax no longer works, because the angular precision needed quickly falls below the noise threshold of our best instruments. That's a fancy way of saying that you can never see a single grass blade at the other end of a football field, even with the best binoculars. Make that distance in light-years instead of yards, and you'll see why astronomers need some other means to figure galactic distances (Hawking, 2001).

There are stellar supernovae of a certain type (Type Ia) that blow up in a very special way. These are stars of a very large mass, and their explosions are so predictable that they are used as "Standard Candles." That term stems from how bright a "standard" candle is when seen from a given distance; this is a scientific hold-over from two centuries ago when people wrote their scientific observations by candle light. The idea is that if something always blows up the same way and gives off the same amount of light each time, then the *dimmer* the light, the *farther away* the source must be – and we can measure how dim the light is up to a certain point. This was perfect for astronomers, because while there are other Cosmic Distance Ladders out there (Cepheid Variables for example), Type Ia supernovae can be seen and measured a whole lot farther away. Think: we can measure even out to very distant galaxies (like a blade of grass over in the next state.)

Hang in with us here, this really is going someplace, we promise.

In the 1930's, astronomer Edwin Hubble (the guy the space telescope was named after) finally figured out that a lot of the "fuzzy" objects visible in early telescopes were really giant galaxies like the Milky Way. This was a pretty humbling observation, because just a century or two earlier, humankind thought we were the center of all creation. With Hubble's discovery, humankind now realized that it occupied a thin layer on a small stony planet in an insignificant solar system in the middle to outer fringes of an average-sized galaxy – and there were billions of galaxies. In fact, there are at least 170 billion galaxies (at least in the visible universe) in one estimate (Gott, et al., 2005). One recent calculation is that there are *two trillion* galaxies in the total universe (https://phys.org/news/2017-01-universe-trillion-galaxies.html). That's quite a come-down from our once lofty self-importance just a century ago.

But Hubble was more fascinated than bothered. He observed that the farther away these galaxies were, the redder was the light coming from them. For anyone who has heard a fire truck's siren pass by them and noticed the tone change, this is called the Doppler Shift (named for Christian Doppler, an Austrian physicist who died in 1853). The equivalent of the passing siren sound dropping in pitch is light turning redder if something is moving away. The faster you go, the lower the pitch, and you can relate those two with a constant number multiplier. If the galaxy was coming _toward_ you, a galaxy would have a *blue* shift... but almost all galaxies had *red* shifts – so they were all receding. In case you're wondering, the nearby Andromeda galaxy is a major exception to this general rule. It is coming *toward* us (its light is slightly bluer), and it's at least as large as our home galaxy. It's eventually going to dance with our Milky Way.

Ever bake a loaf of raisin bread? As the loaf rises, ALL the raisins are moving away from each other in all directions. The farther away that a given pair of raisins were to start with, the faster they move away from each other as the loaf rises.

Galaxies and raisins: pretty much the same thing.

In 1935 it still wasn't certain how big the Hubble Constant was, but Ed took a stab at a guesstimate: something between 40 and 70. In a nicely behaved universe, the Hubble Constant would relate how far something was simply by how red the light coming from it was. In other words, how much the Hydrogen-Alpha absorption line in a given solar spectrum was shifted down into the red range, multiplied by Ed's Number, would tell you how far away the galaxy was in mega-parsecs (a parsec is 3.26 light-years or about 30 trillion kilometers). At that point of time in science history, everyone already had heard of the Big Bang theory, and this seemed to prove that it was the winner over its big rival, the Steady-State theory.

So, think of this: if you could narrow down the Hubble Constant, you could also get a handle on <u>when</u> things started flying apart. The current best calculation of the Hubble Constant is a bit over 73 km/sec/mega-parsec (Reiss et al., 2016). In the last few decades, the age of the universe has been narrowed down to about 13.8 billion years.

What came before that? ***Good question to ask an atheist.***

OK, if things are flying apart, and there is gravity acting on the same things, then the expansion should be slowing down, as gravity exerts its inevitable pull on those things.

This is pretty straightforward physics, right? Some people speculated that when gravity, an attractive force, finally takes over, everything would collapse back onto itself into something called the *Big Crunch*: the End of the Universe.

It turns out that everyone was <u>*way*</u> wrong on that one.

Dark Energy – Something even Bigger

This one is THE Big Boy.

No, there's nothing evil about it. It's just referred to as Dark Energy because astronomers can't see it. They can see its *effects*, however.

And they can infer its size: it is *ginormous*.

Up to 1998, several different groups of astronomers were trying to figure out how fast the expansion of the universe was slowing down: were we gonna go out with a bang (the "Big Crunch") or expand forever with a whimper (alluding to a favorite poet, T.S. Elliot's "The Hollow Men")?

To their mutual astonishment, they discovered that the universe expansion was actually *accelerating*. To do that, of course, requires a *humongous* amount of energy driving it. It's not dense – there is very little per cubic meter – but it fills the universe.

Figuring out what this Dark Energy is preoccupies astronomers and cosmologists more than just about anything else these days. They may not know what it *is*, but they can calculate how *much* of it there is. Remember from a previous chapter that matter and energy are equivalent: $E=Mc^2$. Current data (from a number of published papers) are consistent with this breakdown range for the universe:

71-73 percent Dark Energy

23-25 percent Dark Matter

4-5 percent ordinary matter (you, me, the dirt we stand on, and the stars).

Not sure about you, but this really boggles *our* minds. We told you that it was huge.

It's ***The Biggest Thing of All in the universe – the biggest thing we can <u>indirectly</u> measure, anyway.***

There are a lot of ideas about what Dark Energy is: Perhaps it's the vacuum energy we talked about in a previous chapter? Or possibly we're mistaken in thinking that Einstein's General Relativity applies the same everywhere, and for all times present and past? Or, maybe this is a manifestation of some sort of ultra-light scalar field that has been speculated about by physicists for ages, called "quintessence" (see Caldwell et al., 1998)? We don't know quite what that is, either – and one of us can hear his uber-practical German grandmother snorting her disgust "Psht!" at "such foolishness."

Perhaps the strangest suggestion we've seen (see Frieman, 2011): "Could the observations be telling us that despite the near-isotropy *(translation: looks nearly the same in all directions)* of the cosmic microwave background, the universe is inhomogeneous on large scales and our Milky Way galaxy is located near the center of a very large void?" This sort of foo-foo writing could be called language abuse, and there is a surprisingly large amount of it even in published (quasi-) scientific literature. People with full imaginations are trying to stake out an idea, however bizarre, just in case someone else picks up on it – and then they will become famous. More to the point, cosmologists have known for quite a while that we are NOT in the center of a very large void.

Occam's Razor is a philosophical way of simplifying messy things (see Gauch, 2003). It basically says that when faced with several possible explanations for something, choosing the simplest one is probably where the smart money lies. For us, this would be something different than what you might think.

When someone says they know where life came from – and it was lightning striking a puddle three or four billion years ago – and why we are here in this incredibly large universe with all the physical parameters precisely aligned to permit our existence, and that even *thinking* about this stuff is just random good luck multiplied by 1 with twenty million zeros after it...

...We'd say that they were half-baked raisin bread.

So where is this going? We've both seen a number of different statements by General Authorities of the Church of Jesus Christ of Latter-Day Saints, to the effect that our deceased ancestors are (1) very aware of us and (2) are near us (*Discourses of Brigham Young, p. 376*; *Joseph Fielding Smith, Answers to Gospel Questions, Deseret Book Company, 1958, 2:84–87*; *Discourses of Brigham Young, p. 379*; *D&C 131:7–8*; *Teachings of the Prophet Joseph Smith, p. 326*). They are NOT referring to being in the <u>ground</u> near us, but <u>close around us</u>. If you have ever wondered how this might be, it seems like there's plenty of extra non-baryonic "stuff" in the universe to more than make a place for them. It might also explain why getting a physical body seems to be so incredibly important (Mark 5:8-13) to those who lost the War in Heaven (Revelations 12: 7-8) and are doomed to be live as spirits forever. There is just not that much baryonic matter – especially in the biosphere of worlds – to share around on the large scale that "other worlds" (Hebrews 1:2; D&C 76:23-24) implies. See our previous chapter, "Spirit is Matter," And the next chapter, "Biosphere to Universe Ratio."

Biosphere to Universe Ratio – DNA and Poetry

Density Issues: There really isn't that much we can live on.

There are many clues – the War in Heaven, the evil spirits desperate to enter the Gadarene pig herd (Mark 5:1-20; Matthew 8:28-34; Christ in Mark 1: 27, 34; and 39 are just some of the more obvious), that a physical body is a *Really Important Thing*. It is apparently truly precious, hard to come by – and envied. Some numbers might help us here:

From Ask An Astronomer: (http://curious.astro.cornell.edu/physics/101-the-universe/cosmology-and-the-big-bang/general-questions/579-what-is-the-mass-of-the-universe-intermediate)

According to several studies, the density of matter in the universe is about 3×10^{-30} g/cm^3, (NASA's preferred number for the density of the universe is 9.9×10^{-30} g/cm^3 https://wmap.gsfc.nasa.gov/universe/uni_matter.html). This means that the universe is 300 billion billion billion (NOTE: a British billion = 1,000 American billions) times less dense than water. Note that this includes the contribution of the currently-unknown-but still-measurable Dark Matter. Thus, the density of actually visible, luminous matter (baryonic matter or what we see as stars and galaxies, and the dirt we stand on) is only about one-tenth of the figure given above. This does NOT include the distribution of Dark Energy, which may by itself account for up to 75% of the matter-energy content of the universe and is causing the accelerating expansion of the universe (and earned Nobel Prizes in 2011).

The size of the *observable* universe is about 93 billion light years across (explained in https://en.wikipedia.org/wiki/Observable_universe). Using the above value of density gives a mass (both dark and luminous baryonic matter) of the universe of about 3×10^{56} g, which is roughly 250 billion galaxies the size of the Milky Way. With numbers so large, the definition of "billion" becomes almost irrelevant.

From The Physics Factbook
(https://hypertextbook.com/facts/2001/AmandaMeyer.shtml):

Whittaker, Robert H. Communities and Ecosystems. Toronto: Macmillan, 1970: 83 provides the following:

World Biomass (109 dry tons) total land 1852, total ocean 3.3, total for earth 1855 ... (Rodin, L.E., and N.I. Bazilevich, 1968; Ryther, J.H. 1963; Strickland, J. D. H., 1965; Whittaker, R.H., 1975, among others):

→ 1,855 Pg... one petagram being equivalent to 10^{15} grams.

Sooooo: Biomass of the Earth is ~1.855×10^{18} grams

Mass of the Universe is $\sim 3 \times 10^{56}$ grams

RATIO: 0.62×10^{-38}

That ratio of biomass to the universe is so small it's really difficult to wrap our heads around it. Of course, there is more than one biosphere in the universe; that would be obvious from the Drake Equation*. However, this was understood more than a century earlier by Joseph Smith and other prophets, who repeatedly wrote about other worlds with living beings. These all are clues hinting at the incredible rarity – and thus the high value – of a material body.

As a high-school and college student, one of us (the physicist) wrote poetry. However, his poetry stopped when he was married. Years later, he pondered why. The poetry he wrote came from a deep well of existential atheist emptiness and personal loneliness, which ended when he joined the Church of Jesus Christ and later married his co-author. She's actually the published poet in the family. We both appreciate poetry, recognize it everywhere, and both occasionally pick up and read poetry anthologies.

If you are looking for something in the Biosphere that epitomizes maximum content in the smallest package, you would be hard-pressed to find anything better than DNA. A single sperm cell weighs somewhere in the picogram range. The X chromosome has approximately 153 million base pairs, while the Y chromosome has about 60 million base pairs. We're not even counting the other 24 chromosomes here.

This all brings us back to the crucial concept of density. There is mass density: a cubic centimeter of uranium weighs 19 times more than a cubic centimeter of water. There is energy density: bunker fuel contains a vast amount of chemical energy to efficiently power ships – far more than wind ever could provide, and besides, you won't get caught on a reef in a lee wind if you have a chemically-powered engine. (St. Paul would never have ended up on Malta if he had been on a motor vessel.)

This density issue also figures in the geologic problem of mineral concentration: there is gold (and platinum-group elements, or PGE's, and copper, etc.) everywhere in the Earth's crust. The problem is that their concentration in most places is so low that it is not economic to mine them. Thus, *Economic Geology* is the study of how to (a) *understand* and to (b) <u>find</u> the concentrations of gold (and copper, and PGE's) in the Earth's crust. In other words, to understand the concentrating mechanisms that give rise to ore bodies – and that also in the same process leave chemical and geophysical clues in the surrounding rocks that tell us where to focus our search. This is a non-trivial issue, as some ore deposits are worth billions, tens of billions, and even hundreds of billions of dollars.

Concentrating mechanisms in geology are everywhere: intrusive-driven hydrothermal cells that give us porphyry copper deposits, epigenetic processes that give us some gold deposits, etc. One straightforward example of concentration is gravity-driven accumulation: a placer deposit. From a vast amount of nearly barren rock in Alaska (or Sierra Leone, or Australia, or Venezuela, etc.), materials are weathered out of rock by freeze-thaw cycles, tree roots, water, and wind action. Heavier material tends to collect in topographic lows where flow rates drop – gold prospectors only pan at the inside banks of a river curve, for example. Think: a river is a gold pan writ large. Diamonds are dense, but they are further concentrated and trapped by surfactant conditions such as certain clays associated with those topographic lows. Thus, river dredging for diamonds in Venezuela only happens where a diabase dike crosses the river and weathers to clay in the water. This doesn't require a PhD to figure out, either: most of the successful miners in Venezuela have little or no education and typically wear nylon shorts, flip-flops, and hand-made straw hats and palm-leaf woven backpacks. Yet they can find and then produce up to a kilo of gold in a day using a suction-pump reaching to the river bottom. At the current price of gold, this amounts to nearly US$ 90,000 in his pocket – daily. Most of the concentration already took place naturally, but the last step comes from man's invention of the hydraulic pump and a shaker table.

An interesting side-effect of this gravity concentration process is that if you can find ONE heavy placer mineral, you in effect find ALL of them. They fall out in the same places. Case in point: the induced polarization geophysical process reacts strongly to ilmenite ($FeTiO_3$; https://patentimages.storage.googleapis.com/62/4f/d2/6f2a07051cbbed/US 6236211.pdf) To a towed-streamer electrically pulsing the seafloor, tiny fractions of ilmenite that have collected in long-covered ancient river drainages fairly shout their presence. If you find the ilmenite, you then have already quickly found the platinum-group elements in Union Bay in Sierra Leone – without having to spend a year grid-drilling the bay. Likewise, you will quickly find the gold in the Tanana River of east-central Alaska and the western Yukon this way.

There is one more interesting analogy here. Poetry is that rare concentration of understanding in language – and with good poetry, layers and layers of understanding. A distinguishing characteristic is that all that understanding is concentrated in just a few words – the bright gold flakes standing out in the black fines at the bottom of the gold pan. In other words, there are many different kinds of nuggets in any good poem – there is a bunker fuel's worth of dense energy (word) there. It would be a fun exercise to count the words in recognized poetry and then calculate the ratio of published poetry to all published words reflecting understanding (e.g., not random gibberish) in English or any other language. Rhyme isn't an issue here – it's far easier to rhyme in declined languages like Spanish, Arabic, or Russian than in English. The issue is concentrating the understanding.

Such a comparison may be as small as the ratio of biosphere to baryonic matter. In other words, something rare and precious. We cherish an elegant Haiku. We value a tiny vial of gold flakes. So, we should also cherish and protect our rare and precious human bodies.

* There are many references to the Drake Equation, first introduced by NASA scientist Frank Drake in 1961 at a conference to calculate the number of worlds that would have intelligent life. This was originally intended by Drake to justify setting up a Search for Extra-Terrestrial Intelligence (SETI) effort. There is no direct reference to a paper published by Drake himself. There are probably nearly as many versions of the equation itself, including one by Gene Roddenberry to justify all the inhabited planets in Star Trek. Some indirect references:

Cocconi, G.; Morisson, P. (1959). "Searching for Interstellar Communications" (PDF). Nature. 184 (4690): pp. 844–846. doi:10.1038/184844a0

Burchell, M.J. (2006). "W(h)ither the Drake equation?". International Journal of Astrobiology 5 (3): pp. 243–250. doi:10.1017/S1473550406003107

https://en.wikipedia.org/wiki/Drake_equation

Intelligence, Part I (The Hidden Gems)

There are several flavors.

Many of us have met the brilliant professor type who can't ever seem to find his keys. I knew a professor when I was a student at Berkeley who was a Nobel Laureate. Each day his wife would drive him to the uphill end of the campus (she didn't trust him to drive himself). He would get out and she would yell "Downhill, Owen, downhill!" The campus security guard in his kiosk would pick up on this and kindly direct him towards nearby Leconte Hall. Owen Chamberlain had an incredible gift for making sense of the many particles being discovered in cloud chambers during the 20th century and had found the anti-proton with Emilio Segré that resulted in winning the 1959 Nobel Prize (Nobel Prize, 1959). He had real trouble finding his office, however. This may be an extreme example, but it makes a point: we *all* have gifts, but no human has *all* the gifts. One gift that Owen Chamberlain had in abundance could be called a narrow form of high intelligence.

The twelfth chapter of First Corinthians talks about the many different gifts given to human beings, including wisdom. The Greek word Paul used for this is phronesis (φρόνησις,), which of several related Greek words is distinctive in meaning *practical wisdom or prudence*. We'd like to discuss variations on that one gift – *intelligence* – that we encounter frequently as scientists. ***There is intelligence, and then there is Intelligence.*** And then, there are also *intelligences*, which we will discuss in a subsequent chapter. One way of viewing "intelligence" is through the lens of Intelligence Quotient, or IQ. This is supposed to be a broad indicator of quickness of mind. One of us has given lectures at Oregon MENSA meetings and the experience is not so much *talking* to an audience as *engaging* the audience. They are *very* intelligent people, and *very* aware of it – but equally quick to admit that they are almost all nerds who dress funny, and they say that with evident pride. And no, we are not Mensa members ourselves.

We've seen *mathematical intelligence*, and we've seen *verbal intelligence* – these are theoretically measured by the SAT exam you may painfully remember from high school. We've watched a young man divide one large number by another in his head; he will quickly give the first several digits of the result, then add another decimal place approximately every second until someone gets tired (the interviewer or the videographer). One of the authors has observed the other author unscramble complex word puzzles in milliseconds. The other one of us doesn't even bother to try; it's just too frustrating (his brain is apparently not designed for it). We speculate that what is actually being measured in the SAT test represents perhaps 12 percent to 15 percent of all forms of intelligence.

We've also seen *geographic intelligence* – and you too probably know someone who can navigate in cities or in a wilderness with a natural ease. A shy Navajo boy would quietly sit through my priests' quorum lessons many years ago, never saying a thing. He was as smart as the other young men, but hesitant about speaking in something other than his first language. When we all went camping together in Aravaipa Canyon, however, this kid just lit up. He had a three-dimensional sense of where he was at all times and seemed to be able to walk sideways on the canyon walls. We all watched him in wonder.

There is *emotional intelligence* – also known as "EQ." We suspect most people reading this book have more than a passing acquaintance with the Dilbert comic strip. Many people reading this, along with both authors, have also likely seen the Dilbert world's sort of haphazard, venal form of management in real life. To prevent this sort of thing, the US Office of Personnel Management created the Federal Executive Institute in Charlottesville, VA.

For senior federal managers the FEI is a month-long management boot-camp on steroids (17-hour days for the first 13 consecutive days). The instructors focused hard on what causes management "train-wrecks." They found that the really ghastly management failures all correlated with a leader with low EQ: In other words, a manager, not a leader, someone who didn't care about anyone except him/herself, someone who placed numerical goals above human beings. When this happens, people start working around the manager, and that component of a federal agency would then become increasingly inefficient – until it fell apart. Low EQ meant an inevitable leadership train-wreck.

There is *practical intelligence* – we both know people with and without college degrees who can figure out *anything* and fix *everything*. This goes hand-in-hand with mechanical intelligence (the genius car-mechanic, for instance), and is closely related to geometric intelligence. Some people can easily see things in three and even four dimensions, while we may stare at our car and wonder why it chose to die suddenly in the middle of an interstate bridge.

There is *language intelligence* – we all know people with the gift of tongues. Both authors are close friends with several people who can comfortably speak six very different and difficult languages. There is also *physical intelligence* – the inexplicable things we see in great athletes. A baseball player who bats .300 is one hard-to-explain example. How can the human mind and nervous system react to a baseball approaching their head at 130 meters per second (90 miles per hour)? Some of our Jujitsu students pick up the falls, rolls, and throws unusually quickly. They deal with simulated random attacks smoothly, effortlessly; we shake our heads and just say, "she's a natural." There are many other manifestations of intelligence, and we've just barely scratched the surface here.

If you saw the movie "Rainman" you will understand what a *savant* is: someone who may not be able to do most things you and I take for granted, but who has an incredible gift down inside just waiting to be discovered. When you see or work with someone who seems "slow," be very, *very* careful about making a dismissive judgment. We have known people who speak slowly, measuring their words, and if you err in discounting them, you will make a grave mistake. They are probably smarter than you. In fact, it seems that we all have several forms of intelligence in varying degrees, as Paul observed 2000 years ago. Look, then, to discover the hidden gem in each individual around you. Someone in the next cubicle over, or someone you've known for years may be a genius – and you have just overlooked her all this time.

If so, shame on you.

Intelligence, Part II (The Refiner's Fire)

Getting there is *never* easy.

> 1 Behold, I will send my messenger, and he shall prepare the way
> before me: and the Lord, whom ye seek, shall suddenly come to his
> temple, even the messenger of the covenant, whom ye delight in: behold,
> he shall come, saith the Lord of hosts.
>
> 2 But who may abide the day of his coming? and who shall stand
> when he appeareth? for he is like a refiner's fire, and like fullers' soap:
>
> 3 And he shall sit as a refiner and purifier of silver: and he shall purify
> the sons of Levi, and purge them as gold and silver, that they may offer
> unto the Lord an offering in righteousness. (Malachi 3: 1-3)

When I was 11 years old, my mother remarried after seven years struggling as a working single mom. When I entered seventh grade shortly afterwards, to my parents' surprise (because the parents were not asked beforehand) we were given an IQ test the first day. I had no idea what it was and didn't take it seriously. I DID note that the Christian Brothers, who ran Garces Junior High School in Bakersfield, California, used the results to divide about 70 of us 12-yr-old boys into two classes. It was made abundantly clear that one class was for "dummies." In the class where I ended up, we were initially arrayed in six rows of six chairs each according to this IQ result. I decline to share where I ended up, but it astounded my new step-father, who had assumed up until then that I was mildly retarded. Two years later this led to the first of several huge changes in my life.

My new step-father badgered my mother for most of that intervening time into letting me go to a public high school, and more importantly, the one public high school in Bakersfield, California, which had a college prep program and an advanced college-prep program. This was like "AP" classes these days, and was the beginning of the Elitist Age, before people figured out that it was probably not wise to discourage growing children by classifying them too early. It was also before educators really came to grips with the fact that there are many, many different forms or manifestations of intelligence.

Why did my mother resist? She had been taught from childhood by Irish Catholic nuns that if she didn't raise her kids Catholic, she would go to Hell. She understood that to be literally the case. It wasn't until after I earned a PhD in geophysics that my mom confided to me that when she married my step-dad, they *both* thought I was mildly retarded. They had correlated my C-average grades with brains. My worst grade was nearly always "Deportment," where a good grade for me was a "C-minus" and a typical grade was a "D-minus." Bored and always in trouble is the short version.

Over time I took other "qualifying" tests; from one of these I gleaned a number off of a file I glimpsed on a high school counselor's desk. I knew enough by then to realize that this was a really good number. For a short while, I reveled in this number.

> *"If a person gains more knowledge and intelligence in this life through his diligence and obedience... he will have so much the advantage in the world to come" (D&C 130:19).*

But the difference in intelligence between someone 12 years old and someone 27 years old could be measured in light-years. I struggled very hard through grad school. When my PhD committee came out of the discussion room, one at a time, each shook my hand and said solemnly, "Congratulations, *DOCTOR* Wynn." The last one sauntered out of the conference room, shook my hand, and said: *"Now you can finally start learning."* Boy, ain't that the truth.

But here's a secret: that intelligence initially gifted to you can (and probably will) increase in quantum steps as you get older – but only if you work at it. The downside is that you have to go through the worm-hole to get to the next quantum state. That's a physicist's way of saying you get there by spending months to years in a kind of Living Hell (like grad school, or Basic Training). It's also called the Refiner's Fire. You can delay some of this, you can even waste much of your life trying to avoid it, but a loving God will be very persistent in "allowing" you to have opportunities that, once past them, you will be grateful for. If you're like me, however, you would never willingly go back to go through those hard experiences again.

I once visited a gold mine in Saudi Arabia called Mahd ad-Dhahab (the name means "cradle of gold" in Arabic). There I watched the hard-rock blasting, the ore transport, the milling, crushing, and grinding process, the dense-liquid floating separation, the huge, yellow-hot smelter – and finally I held a brick of doré in my hands: a block of ~97 percent pure gold. It took both hands, too, because something solid gold the size of a smallish red building brick weighed about 30 kilos (70 pounds).

I traced back in my mind the process to get to this point and saw a metaphor for human life. Every crucible we are poured from leaves us better and smarter: smarter in empathy, smarter in patience, smarter in understanding, smarter in parenthood.

That last one has also made me smarter at understanding who I am, why I am here, and Who will welcome me back Home.

Intelligence, Part III (Intelligences *plural*)

Starting to understand who we really are.

> *"Man was also in the beginning with God. Intelligence, or the light of truth, was not created or made, neither indeed can be".* (D&C 93:29)

In the scriptures of the Church of Jesus Christ, that single verse has <u>five</u> qualifying links or footnotes. Here is a totally different take on the word "intelligence" – and this version is usually found in the plural: *Intelligences.*

Almost everyone I have ever talked with will agree on one thing: they know things from somewhere that they can't explain. For instance, I may mention the concept of marriage that lasts beyond death, or the idea of a pre-existence. They all say something like "Yeah, I know that…" even when I point out that it is inconsistent with the tenets of their particular faith.

Catholic priests are viewed by their parishioners as intercessors because they explain the incomprehensible things in the Bible to plain folk like you and me. But here's something – existence before we were born – that my Jesuit friend Father Fulco was unable to explain to me:

> *"Before I formed thee in the belly I knew thee; and before thou camest forth out of the womb I sanctified thee, and I ordained thee a prophet unto the nations".* (**Jeremiah 1:5**)

Where did I come from? Why am I here? Where am I going? – These are the only really important questions for us as individuals.

As we now understand it, we have already existed for billions of years – The Lord in Jeremiah is referring to a *Pre-Existence.* This certainly would explain that pre-existing memory that everyone seems to have. Here's another one:

> *"Intelligence was not created or made"* (D&C 93:29).

The first time we heard this in a Sunday school class it surprised us, but again, that pre-existent memory said, "Yeah – of course." So… we weren't created, we were *organized* into existence as individual beings, and we were given agency. But we had already existed in some form before that.

Now *there's* something to occupy your windshield thoughts during a long commuter trip.

How? We don't know for certain – at least not in any detail – but the now well-established existence of vast amounts of dark matter and dark energy (and also vacuum energy and quantum entanglement) sure seem like bright, neon-lit clues. These vast amounts of energy and matter persistently come to mind when alone on that long drive; how they might fit in certainly opens up tantalizing possibilities. What if this baryonic matter (the electrons, protons, neutrons, etc. that we are made of) is in rather short supply? Current cosmological evidence tells us that "we" and the visible universe around us apparently make up just 4-5 percent of that universe (see the previous chapter on Dark Energy). How does this figure into the larger equation? There are several possibilities that might explain the tantalizing hints in the Doctrine and Covenants and the Pearl of Great Price. If we all live right, and ponder these hints, we are both convinced that the answers will come.

You have probably noticed by now that several times we have discussed non-baryonic matter... that is, all the rest of the "stuff" in this universe other than us, the dirt we stand on, and the stars. We spent a lot of time developing this information for you in previous chapters for several compelling reasons. The very fact that everything we can actually touch and shovel and see constitutes just 4+ percent of what is around us in this universe... is very sobering (see our previous chapter, "Biosphere to Universe Ratio – DNA and Poetry"). The biology-hosting part of the Earth is only 0.0000000003 of the Earth as a whole. The number would be far smaller if we tried to ratio the biosphere to the entire Solar System, but we hope you get the point: Where humans can live in this universe is an incredibly tiny fraction of the universe as a whole. This should *really* demand our attention. While we can provide numbers for the Earth, they're really meaningless as we don't know what the habitability of exoplanets might be, even within 20 light years of our Sun – but since the 1830's we have known that other habitable worlds *do exist*.

We suspect that the astonishingly tiny ratio of biosphere-to-universe could go a long way towards explaining a number of things: why having a physical body is so very, very precious – why a WAR was fought around the issue. It might help explain why we can't occupy our bodies for too long (we living humans are already stretching the food and water limits of our planet as we write this). And it might even explain where all the people including parents and grandparents who have gone before us *now* *dwell*... but can still remain very close to us. And perhaps why we can sometimes sense their near presence. It might also help us better understand why we instinctively want to have spirit and matter together, and why we want to "hear" more of what is going on in that Other Side. And finally, why it powerfully touches us when we *do*.

We believe we are almost at the point where we can understand and begin to tie all these tantalizing cosmological and scriptural pieces together. It's another reason not to fear death. Beyond *that* door, this learning thing just *has* to speed up dramatically. We won't need sleep or sugar, among other things. And we will have full access to *all* of those pre-existent memories.

How cool is that?!

Can a Good Christian Believe in Evolution?

We've watched 60-cm (2-ft) rats shinny up steel bars, and fly over 2-meter (6-ft) cinder-block walls. It's increasingly difficult to argue with evolution in your face.

A friend recently asked us this question. "Doesn't the Bible say Adam and Eve were created as the first man and woman and placed in the Garden of Eden? So how can you believe that those fossils of humans that supposedly lived before Adam and Eve did were really humans? And how can you believe in the story of the creation, and still think that Adam and Eve evolved from something else before that?"

Good question! Some people try simply to avoid reconciling their understanding of the Bible with the current version of science by not thinking about it. They essentially, as Henry Eyring, Sr., once said, "...keep their religion in one pocket and their science in another." (Eyring, 1972; 1983).

Maybe they're afraid that they'll lose their testimony. And, certainly, scientific ideas are sometimes expressed as if there is a contest between religion and science, with the winner's success leaving the loser without any followers. Now, *that's* sure a zero-sum approach!

But it's not a contest, not a battle, and we don't have to avoid thinking about science and religion. We can easily maintain our integrity as believers in (understanders of) the Bible while still thinking about what science has taught us since the Bible was written.

In fact, we don't think God expects us to avoid thinking about science (or *anything*), even when science appears to show evidence contradictory to some Biblical teaching. From everything we have read, we are certain that God wants us to keep learning as much as we can about this magnificent Earth that He has created for us while we keep worshiping Him.

There is no official Church position on evolution, so do not confuse the personal opinions of some church leaders on this subject with Church doctrine. Often, it's *not*. The church's official documents on the theory of evolution do not appear to contradict the idea that hominids could have existed before Adam and Eve were placed in the Garden of Eden.

Here's one, a 1925 First Presidency letter, which reads, in part:

> *"'God created man in his own image, in the image of God created he him: male and female created he them.'*

"In these plain and pointed words the inspired author of the book of Genesis made known to the world the truth concerning the origin of the human family. Moses, the prophet-historian, who was "learned" we are told, "in all the wisdom of the Egyptians," when making this important announcement, was not voicing a mere opinion. He was speaking as the mouthpiece of God, and his solemn declaration was for all time and for all people."

The letter doesn't say whether any human-like creatures existed before that. And it doesn't have to, does it? President Harold B. Lee has pointed out that we don't know enough about the details of God's creation of the Earth and its inhabitants to compare it with evolutionary theory:

"Perhaps if we had the full story of the creation of the earth and man told to us in great detail, it would be more of a mystery than the simple few statements that we have contained in the Bible, because of our lack of ability to comprehend. Therefore, for reasons best known to the Lord, He has kept us in darkness. Wait until the Lord speaks, or wait until that day when He shall come, and when we shall be among the privileged either to come up out of our graves and be caught up into the clouds of heaven or shall be living upon the earth likewise to be so translated before Him. Then we shall know all things pertaining to this earth, how it was made, and all things that now as children we are groping for and trying to understand."

More recently, President Gordon B. Hinckley wrote, "What the Church requires is only belief that Adam was the first man of what we would call the human race. Scientists can speculate on the rest." (Gordon B. Hinckley in 2002; cited in Jarvik, 2006). See also (Stephens and Meldrum, 2001).

Finally, this wonderful quote by Hugh Nibley:

Do not begrudge existence to creatures that looked like men long, long ago, nor deny them a place in God's affection or even a right to exaltation — for our scriptures allow them such. Nor am I overly concerned as to just when they might have lived, for their world is not our world. They have all gone away long before our people ever appeared. God assigned them their proper times and functions, as he has given me mine — a full-time job that admonishes me to remember his words to the overly eager Moses: "For mine own purpose have I made these things. Here is wisdom and it remaineth in me." (Moses 1:31) It is Adam as my own parent who concerns me. When he walks onto the stage, then and only then the play begins. (Nibley, 1986).

So, until such time as we know "all things pertaining to this earth, how it was made, and all things that now as children we are groping for and trying to understand," why not keep learning everything we can about what science knows so far?

Because, as a Church of Jesus Christ scientist who has published many articles about science and Church beliefs writes (Lawrence Berkeley Lab researcher David H. Bailey, who spoke at the Science and Mormonism symposium in Provo in November 2013 via Skype from the New Zealand Temple):

> *"The <LDS Church> has a great scientific tradition, including notable, respected researchers in virtually every field of modern science. Indeed, our motto is 'The glory of God is intelligence' (Interpreter Foundation, 2013).*

"Why not just acknowledge that science and religion address two very different sets of questions, and that the methodology in one arena cannot settle controversies in the other?"

Evolution and the Biblical Creation Account

What if we – and the Bible – have *both* evolved?

We've also been asked how a practicing Christian can accept the idea of the evolution of species when the Bible specifically says that God commanded the earth to "bring forth the living creature after his kind, cattle, and creeping thing, and beast of the earth after his kind: and it was so" (Genesis 1:23). *THAT* wording is actually exactly consistent with evolution!

And, of course, the question of the age of the Earth as derived from geological evidence from all over the world, complete with fossils from animals that lived hundreds of millions of years ago, is contradicted by traditionalist ideas about the age of the Earth as "calculated" from Biblical accounts. This assumes that the Bible is perfect and inspired, of course. History again comes to our aid, in the form of extensive scholarly documentation on how the Bible and its various canons evolved over time through multiple languages. There are many different versions of the Bible, with different content; there is even a King James Version that includes this verse in the Ten Commandments "Thou shalt commit adultery." As you might guess, this version is referred to as the "Wicked Bible" (Campbell, 2010).

More to the point, the idea of Biblical inerrancy – that the KJV is perfect and inspired by God – *is something that didn't appear in western culture until the late 19th Century* (Campbell, 2010). So again, we see that history is critical for evaluating errant claims in both science *and* religion.

This information is useful at many different levels. One of us had a religion teacher while in high school who seriously told us that dinosaur bones were put on Earth by God to test us: If we believed they were evidence of the long haul of evolution, we had insufficient faith. If we believed in the Bible's account of the Creation, we would know that those fossils were not evidence of evolution, or of an ancient origin of Earth's history and species.

We raise this because we know many people have been raised with this same hard dichotomy. They have been led to believe that you have to either accept that interpretation of the (KJV) Bible's account or accept the evidence of science – and there is nothing in between. For them there is no other acceptable interpretation of the Bible except that it is inerrant, and no possibility that science can be anything other than a trick to fool us and rob us of our beliefs. For others, it's the opposite: religious traditionalists are uneducated. Some scientists have tried to have both extremes at the same time. As Henry Eyring once said some religious scientists feel they have to "...keep their religion in one pocket and their science in another" (Eyring, 1972). Don Lind, the NASA astronaut, said something similar to this, quoted at the beginning of this book (Lind, 1973).

But there is no contest between religion and science, with the winner's success leaving the other side a loser without any followers. That's a historically recent, very artificial, and frankly myopic dichotomy. True religion and true science are not in conflict, despite the way that some scientists sometimes express scientific ideas – and despite the way some religious people express religious beliefs. We can maintain our integrity as believers in the Bible while still thinking about what science has taught us since the Bible was written. Remember, the Bible was written down by shepherds in the language of shepherds, not in the language of cosmologists.

In fact, God nowhere requires us to avoid thinking about science (or anything!), even when science appears to show apparent "evidence" contradictory to some Biblical teaching. We are convinced that God wants us to use the brains He gave us, and keep learning as much as we can about this magnificent Earth He has created for us.

Meanwhile, we are enriched by additional accounts of God's creation of the Earth in the Book of Abraham and Book of Moses, both of which indicate a kind of spiritual creation, or template for creation, before the actual physical creation of the Earth and its creatures. See, for instance, Abraham 4:18-26, in which we read about "the Gods" not "creating" but "ordering" all the things that happen during what we call the creation, waiting and watching those things "until they obeyed"; "prepar[ing] the earth" to bring forth the animals and then "organiz[ing] the earth until they "saw they would obey"; and finally talking about going down to create humans and then going down to "organize" them.

Likewise, in the Book of Moses, we read:

And now, behold, I say unto you, that these are the generations of the heaven and of the earth, when they were created, in the day that I, the Lord God, made the heaven and the earth,

And every plant of the field before it was in the earth, and every herb of the field before it grew. For I, the Lord God, created all things, of which I have spoken, spiritually, before they were naturally upon the face of the earth. For I, the Lord God, had not caused it to rain upon the face of the earth. And I, the Lord God, had created all the children of men; and not yet a man to till the ground; for in heaven created I them; and there was not yet flesh upon the earth, neither in the water, neither in the air (Moses 3:4-5)

Finally, in Abraham 4:31, the Gods (note that the plural of God is also in Genesis) say,

"We will do everything that we have said, and organize them; and behold, they shall be very obedient. And it came to pass that it was from evening until morning they called night; and it came to pass that it was from morning until evening that they called day; and they numbered the sixth time."

Note the use of the word "day" here. In the King James Version, the word translated as "day," as in "on the first day," and so on, doesn't necessarily mean one 24-hour period. In fact, the Hebrew word "yom" can also mean a general, vague time (as we ourselves sometimes use the word "day"); some unspecified point of time (as in "In Joseph's day"); a period of light (usually a 24-hour day); and there are additional meanings, just as there are when we use the English word "day." Some Biblical references actually refer to a day being a thousand years (see Psalm 90:4 and II Peter 3:8).

Back to the creation. Moses 3 and 4 make it clear that what we call "the creation" is actually a planning council followed by a protracted process of organizing and structuring matter that already existed. Beginning in Moses 2:2, we read:

And the earth was without form, and void; and I caused darkness to come up upon the face of the deep; and my Spirit moved upon the face of the water; for I am God.

And I, God, said: Let there be light; and there was light.

And I, God, saw the light; and that light was good. And I, God, divided the light from the darkness (Moses 2:2-4).

Finally, the first verse of chapter 5 says,

"And thus we will finish the heavens and the earth, and all the hosts of them."

Ah! So, it *was* a planning meeting. The actual time it will take to do all those things is not specified, as time itself had not been created yet. It is created and periods of time are named now:

And I, God, called the light Day; and the darkness, I called Night; and this I did by the word of my power, and it was done as I spake; and the evening and the morning were the first day (Moses 2:5).

But, you may say, "These are just Church of Jesus Christ-specific accounts. Of course, they're going to be different." Yet in the Old Testament itself there are other accounts of the creation, including one in the 104th Psalm. We know of the "Yahweh" and the "Elohim" accounts which appear side by side right in Genesis (see, for example, the discussion of these two accounts at http://apologeticspress.org/apcontent.aspx?category=6&article=1131), as well as many other ancient creation accounts (for instance, see "List of creation myths" on Wikipedia, https://en.wikipedia.org/wiki/List_of_creation_myths, to get an idea of the number and variety of these accounts.)

And, remember that members of the Church of Jesus Christ acknowledge what many other Christian sects do not – it's stated right in the Eighth Article of Faith:

We believe the Bible to be the word of God as far as it is translated correctly; we also believe the Book of Mormon to be the word of God.

So, let's turn full circle to where we started: The Church of Jesus Christ does not preach "creationist" ideas. On the contrary, as already noted, the methodology of science cannot help in religious matters, and vice-versa. As Church members, we do not make arguments that, for instance, evolution has never been observed (it has been observed, and abundantly, including by both authors); that evolution violates the second law of thermodynamics (it doesn't); that there are no transitional fossils (there are and in abundance, and even if there weren't that would not prove anything); that because the theory of evolution is called a "theory," it is somehow just an idea that hasn't been and can't be proved (it has been tested and proven repeatedly at all levels); or that Darwin's theory of evolution claims that life originated, and evolution proceeds, by random chance (it doesn't make that claim).

First, evolution has been observed in many instances. These include microbes that develop resistance to antibiotics; in changing variants of the influenza virus from year to year as vaccines are developed to fight each new version; and even in larger, more complex organisms, as when humans breed new varieties of plants and even animals. An example of this is Russian selective breeding of silver foxes to become more like dogs in color variations and friendly behavior. (An interesting overview of this study is available online at Goldman, 2010).

Second, evolution does not violate the second law of thermodynamics. This law states that order eventually becomes disorder as energy is lost from the system. But Earth is not a closed system; energy is constantly being re-supplied from the sun, so order is maintained and even increased, as primitive organisms become more complex. Even non-living objects show an increase in order from a disordered state. Snowflakes, sand dunes, tornadoes, stalactites, graded river beds, and lightning are just a few examples of order coming from disorder in nature.

Third, thousands of transitional fossils have been uncovered since the Paleozoic Era began. The fossil record is still very incomplete and always will be; erosion and the conditions favorable to fossilization make this inevitable. But the record is still there.

Fourth, when we talk about Darwin's "theory" of evolution, we don't mean "theory" in the sense of some idea that needs to be proven. Instead, it is a "theory" in the sense that it raises questions and proposes solutions that can be tested and found to be true or false. And over time it has been shown to be a correct and workable explanation for the variations we see in nature; and

Fifth, Darwin's theory of evolution does not claim that evolution began or continues by random chance. Darwin doesn't make any claims about how the first life came about, only that once it was here, it changed (evolved) through natural selection.

Consider: About a hundred years ago, scientists, who were then mostly creationists, looked at the world to figure out how God worked. These creationists came to the conclusions of an old Earth, and species originating by evolution. Since then, thousands of scientists have been studying evolution with increasingly more sophisticated tools. Most of these scientists have excellent understandings of the laws of thermodynamics, how fossil finds are interpreted, etc., and finding a better alternative to evolution would win them fame and fortune. Sometimes their work has changed our understanding of significant details of how evolution operates, but evolution still has essentially unanimous agreement from the people who work in science, believers or not, including the entire biology faculty of Brigham Young University (Science and Mormonism Symposium, Provo, UT, November 2011).

Because true religion (from the Latin *re+ligare*, or re-connect) and true science (from the Latin *scientia*, or knowledge) are both seeking truth, they ought to be united. That's in fact the whole point of this book. As long as either side puts on blinders and chooses to argue against a misunderstanding of the other side's beliefs, no common ground on which to continue the discussion will be found.

Darwin and Christianity

Darwin was *NOT* an Atheist. But it doesn't really matter, does it?

Private
Nov. 24 1880
Dear Sir,
I am sorry to have to
inform you that I do
not believe in the Bible
as a divine revelation
& therefore not in Jesus
Christ as the son of God.
Yours faithfully
Ch. Darwin

This letter, written in 1880, seems to show that Darwin himself no longer believed in God or in the Christian religion of his time. Therefore, some atheists tell us, there is no reason for any of us to believe in the Bible, in God, nor in Jesus Christ as the son of God.

There are other indications that Darwin found the Christianity taught in England in his time not to be believable. For instance, Darwin wrote to his American collaborator, Asa Gray:

> With respect to the theological view of the question; this is always painful to me. — I am bewildered. — I had no intention to write atheistically. But I own that I cannot see, as plainly as others do, & as I [should] wish to do, evidence of design & beneficence on all sides of us. There seems to me too much misery in the world. I cannot persuade myself that a beneficent & omnipotent God would have designedly created the Ichneumonidæ with the express intention of their feeding within the living bodies of caterpillars, or that a cat should play with mice. Not believing this, I see no necessity in the belief that the eye was expressly designed. On the other hand I cannot anyhow be contented to view this wonderful universe & especially the nature of man, & to conclude that everything is the result of brute force. I am inclined to look at everything as resulting from designed laws, with the details, whether good or bad, left to the working out of what we may call chance (https://www.darwinproject.ac.uk/letter/DCP-LETT-2814.xml).

Does this indicate that Darwin has become a nonbeliever? We don't think so. In fact, as he continues in this passage:

"I feel most deeply that the whole subject is too profound for the human intellect. A dog might as well speculate on the mind of Newton.— Let each man hope & believe what he can."

(https://www.darwinproject.ac.uk/letter/DCP-LETT-2814.xml)

Not only does Darwin NOT seem to us to have become an atheist, but he seems to be simply puzzling out the conflicts between his scientific observations and conclusions on the one hand, and the teachings of mainstream, post-Nicaean Christian orthodoxy of his time, on the other.

Darwin's conclusions and writings about his work inspired seven Anglican religious leaders to publish a "manifesto," *Essays and Reviews*, in which they argued that the Bible stories should not be interpreted literally but as myths. This "manifesto" was condemned in 1861 by the Church of England. (https://www.episcopalchurch.org/library/glossary/essays-and-reviews).

In Darwin's autobiography, he continued to consider how Christianity and other religious beliefs fit in with objective, rational, scientific observations. He struggled with the "problem of evil" in the traditional Christian view and wrote that the more he knew "of the fixed laws of nature the more incredible do miracles become," and added that "disbelief crept over me at a very slow rate, but was at last complete. The rate was so slow that I felt no distress, and have never since doubted even for a single second that my conclusion was correct."

Here's an example of how Darwin worked through the problem of belief:

With respect to the theological view of the question; this is always painful to me.— I am bewildered.— I had no intention to write atheistically. But I own that I cannot see, as plainly as others do, & as I sh^d wish to do, evidence of design & beneficence on all sides of us. There seems to me too much misery in the world. I cannot persuade myself that a beneficent & omnipotent God would have designedly created the Ichneumonidæ with the express intention of their feeding within the living bodies of caterpillars, or that a cat should play with mice. Not believing this, I see no necessity in the belief that the eye was expressly designed. On the other hand I cannot anyhow be contented to view this wonderful universe & especially the nature of man, & to conclude that everything is the result of brute force. I am inclined to look at everything as resulting from designed laws, with the details, whether good or bad, left to the working out of what we may call chance. Not that this notion at all satisfies me. I feel most deeply that the whole subject is too profound

*for the human intellect. A dog might as well speculate on the mind of
Newton.— Let each man hope & believe what he can.—*

*Certainly I agree with you that my views are not at all necessarily
atheistical. The lightning kills a man, whether a good one or bad one,
owing to the excessively complex action of natural laws,—a child (who
may turn out an idiot) is born by action of even more complex laws,—and
I can see no reason, why a man, or other animal, may not have been
aboriginally produced by other laws; & that all these laws may have been
expressly designed by an omniscient Creator, who foresaw every future
event & consequence. But the more I think the more bewildered I become;
as indeed I have probably shown by this letter. (Letter to Asa Gray, 22
May 1860: https://www.darwinproject.ac.uk/letter/?docId=letters/DCP-
LETT-2814.xml;query=wonderful%20universe;brand=default)*

In our reading, then, he called himself "agnostic" in the sense of
"not knowing," or "not being sure," rather than in the sense we usually
think of "agnostic" now, as someone who has abandoned religious beliefs
but hasn't yet embraced atheism. In 1879, he reaffirmed this view:

*"In my most extreme fluctuations I have never been an atheist in the
sense of denying the existence of a God.— I think that generally (& more
and more so as I grow older) but not always, that an agnostic would be
the most correct description of my state of mind."* (Letter to John
Fordyce, 7 May 1879:
https://www.darwinproject.ac.uk/letter/?docId=letters/DCP-LETT-
12041.xml;query=agnostic;brand=default)

Thus, when atheists seized upon his work as evidence that their
view is the only correct one, he wrote:

*"...though I am a strong advocate for free thought on all subjects, yet
it appears to me (whether rightly or wrongly) that direct arguments
against Christianity & theism produce hardly any effect on the public; &
freedom of thought is best promoted by the gradual illumination of men's
minds, which follows from the advance of science. It has, therefore, been
always my object to avoid writing on religion, & I have confined myself to
science. I may, however, have been unduly biased by the pain which it
would give some members of my family, if I aided in any way direct
attacks on religion."* (Letter to E.B. Aveling, 13 October 1880:
https://www.darwinproject.ac.uk/letter/?docId=letters/DCP-LETT-
12757.xml;query=freedom%20of%20thought;brand=default)

On the other hand, he also wrote:

"I can indeed hardly see how anyone ought to wish Christianity to be true; for if so the plain language of the text seems to show that the men who do not believe, and this would include my Father, Brother and almost all my best friends, will be everlastingly punished. And this is a damnable doctrine.

"The old argument of design in nature, as given by Paley, which formerly seemed to me so conclusive, fails, now that the law of natural selection had been discovered. We can no longer argue that, for instance, the beautiful hinge of a bivalve shell must have been made by an intelligent being, like the hinge of a door by man. There seems to be no more design in the variability of organic beings and in the action of natural selection, than in the course which the wind blows. Everything in nature is the result of fixed laws.

"At the present day (ca. 1872) the most usual argument for the existence of an intelligent God is drawn from the deep inward conviction and feelings which are experienced by most persons. But it cannot be doubted that Hindoos, Mahomadans and others might argue in the same manner and with equal force in favor of the existence of one God, or of many Gods, or as with the Buddhists of no God...This argument would be a valid one if all men of all races had the same inward conviction of the existence of one God: but we know that this is very far from being the case. Therefore I cannot see that such inward convictions and feelings are of any weight as evidence of what really exists."

He wrote in a letter to F.E. Abbot, dated 6 September 1871:

My views are far from clear, as you will readily perceive if you will will read the last page in my Variation of Animals & Plants under Domestication. 4 I can never make up my mind how far an inward conviction that there must be some Creator or First Cause is really trustworthy evidence. Moreover I have been for the last six weeks much out of health with giddiness & other head-symptoms, & do not feel equal to deep reflexion on the deepest subject which can fill a man's mind. In fact I have only during the last few days been able to do anything of any sort. —

(https://www.darwinproject.ac.uk/letter/?docId=letters/DCP-
LETT-7924.xml;query=First%20Cause;brand=default)

What can we make of all this? Darwin made the same observations that believers in the restored gospel of Jesus Christ accept.

While we believe the Bible to be the word of God, we add, "as long as it is translated correctly" (8th Article of Faith).

We believe all that God has revealed AND that He will yet reveal many more beautiful truths about the earth and all its flora and fauna, including humans and their relations with God (9th Article of Faith].

We believe that not everything in the form of the Biblical translations we have available to us now is correct; and that there are many other historical sacred records that will be brought forth in the future; and that these, without the intervening centuries of translation and doctrinal errors, will explain a lot of the theology that we don't understand now.

While we believe that all mankind may be saved by obedience to the laws and ordinances of the gospel of Jesus Christ, we understand that truth is not found only in "our" church; we see, as Darwin did, that Hindus' and Muslims' and Buddhists' versions of God, godliness, divine nature, or strivings to divinity also have much light and truth in them.

We believe in a loving and kind God whose ways are beyond our own, so far beyond our own that we can't even imagine all of His purposes. We believe that even the most evil and sinful humans and horrible deeds throughout history have been foreseen by God, have been allowed to do their work and innocents allowed to suffer, not because God is uncaring or evil in any way; if we saw the true and actual consequences of all our behaviors and all the sufferings in the world, as God does, we would understand. But God honors our free agency, even in the breach, and with His broader vision sees our time on this Earth as a short interlude given to us to contrast with – and therefore allow us to appreciate more – the Eternal Life that follows.

We think it is folly, at best, to attempt to second-guess the Organizer of this universe, His works, His love, His teachings, or any of His interactions with humans. It is even more foolish to believe that an evolving science is suddenly fixed, finally, on all truth... and can now magically explain all creation and the origin of life.

Darwin tried throughout his life to *work out his salvation with fear and trembling* [Philippians 2:12], as both a scientist and a thoughtful human being. He refused to let atheists claim him as one of their own. For us, Darwin exemplifies a true scientist in his persistent honesty – and his frequent recognition that science itself is an evolving process. He readily acknowledged that he couldn't even begin to comprehend the creation and organization of the vast universe surrounding us, and he acknowledged his and all humanity's limitations in understanding the Hand of God.

(To read more on your own about Darwin's scientific observations and how they affected his religious understandings, go to The Darwin Project: https://www.darwinproject.ac.uk/)

What has History got to do with Science and Religion?

Can science learn anything from history?

Honesty. The short answer is that it forces honesty among most scientists. Here's the longer answer:

When someone demands "objective evidence" for something in the past, they are naïve at best. The past doesn't exist and cannot ever be directly observed by us. Anything that we read about it must necessarily be viewed with some level of suspicion because anything written will inevitably contain some degree of bias and external agenda (see the chapter "Victor's History, Skewed History"). You cannot conduct experiments on history: it is a non-empirical discipline. Therefore, any demand for "objective evidence" of say, the Book of Mormon, or the Bible, represents a fundamental misunderstanding of the nature of human history. Archeologists and geographers have found a number of things that support the historicity of both the Bible and the Book of Mormon, but anyone who claims to prove or disprove either has not read very much.

However, the history of science is still a powerful and important tool for evaluating science and assessing its progress. The philosophy of science is especially important because it enforces logic and honesty.

History is crucial to our understanding that science is a fundamentally human endeavor, always evolving, and like all human efforts (a) builds on previous work, and (b) progresses in an uneven manner. Science, for instance, must start somewhere. For physicists and cosmologists this means accepting a priori the physical laws of the universe, the Big Bang, and the Anthropic Principle. They cannot question these, as Bertrand Russell pointed out – "The universe is just there, and that's all" (Russell and Copleston, 1964). They can no longer be questioned, there is so much evidence supporting them. However, while the timing and early phases of the Big Bang can be evaluated theoretically, they cannot be studied empirically. What preceded the Big Bang can never be viewed (the Cosmic Microwave Background only hints at what happened AFTER the Big Bang). There is no way to objectively pass through the singularity of the Big Bang and view its predecessor. Likewise, the physical constants in our universe are just there: the Anthropic Principle cannot be questioned either; it can only be accepted. Science starts somewhere after these are (whether humbly or brusquely) accepted.

It is also critically important to make a sharp distinction between science and technology here – they are often confabulated, and the wonders of modern electronics and space vehicles commonly lead even highly educated scientists into believing that their work represents the ultimate truth. *History tells us otherwise.* The early Greeks understood a solar-centric planetary system, but this understanding was lost for millennia. Scientists, until 1965, taught us that cigarette smoking aided digestion after dinner. Scientists until 50 years ago taught us that our Earth was in a steady state; plate tectonics were not really accepted until after 1970. Science teaches us a lot about cancer – but just wait another 20 years.

We have been talking in this book about the differences between religion, philosophy, and science, and how they are all different paths to a larger truth. However, we must add history to this troika, though with the provisions above. All four of these disciplines (for want of a better word) have in common the search for Truth with a capital "T" – that is, the search for knowledge that stands the test of time. *None of them, by themselves, can currently provide us everything.*

As we mentioned earlier, the history of science is crucial to understanding both the strengths and limitations of science. We can learn – and also become better at our own truth-hunting – by watching the scientific approach as it has so far been applied to our understanding of physics, biology, geology, and essentially every field of science. Reading about Mendel, Lyell and Hutton, Darwin and Wallace, and all those pioneers of our current understanding of the development of our planet and the creatures that dwell on it, is fascinating. We can see the work of researchers be challenged and tested, perhaps confirmed and perhaps supplanted (and like Lysenko, their names forgotten), and we are elated at the progress we've made and excited for what is still to come. But we cannot allow ourselves the luxury of thinking that we are there yet – or even almost there. History will – or should – keep us humble.

For our purposes, we need to distinguish between the methods and capabilities of science and history. To do this we need to separate disciplines within what we usually call history: for instance, the study of ancient inscriptions, even when they are found in archaeological digs, is different from the study of those archaeological sites themselves. Skeletons with syphilitic lesions tell us more than any history book will. If we looked only at the inscriptions that Rameses the Great erected commemorating his great "victory" at the Battle of Kadesh, we would miss the crucial point that it was actually a terrible disaster, and that Rameses barely escaped with his life, and only by sacrificing his personal Ra troops bodyguard (Grimal, 1992).

Finally, we need to distinguish between the goals, methods, and capabilities of science and history as compared to those of philosophy and religion.

History and Historicity

There *IS* a difference.

The historicity of the Bible (how much can be correlated with history from other sources) has been worked on by scholars for at least two centuries; the *Journal of Biblical Archaeology* is a good starting place to learn more about this. A *very* small part of the contents of the Bible (such as references to Assyrian kings, etc.) can be correlated with archeological observations. *Virtually no conversations can be validated.*

The Bible took place in an arid environment with some mild tectonism, but largely devoid of volcanism – in other words, an environment conducive to the preservation of records. Cuneiform tablets and the Dead Sea Scrolls come to mind here. Even then, most writing on any other media was not preserved unless repeatedly copied onto new scrolls over millennia.

What about the historicity of the Book of Mormon? The first 17 chapters of the Book of Mormon are remarkably consistent with archaeology of the eastern Mediterranean and Arabian Peninsula. The Uto-Aztecan language group has over 1,500 cognates and linguistic structures in common with central and south Arabian Semitic languages (Stubbs, 2016). However, looking for physical Book of Mormon evidence in Central America, as many have done, is a losing proposition because it is a very different environment. With the exception of very large stone edifices and a few painted murals, almost nothing written has survived the Pre-classic Mayan period (500 BC to roughly 250 AD, roughly coincident with the Book of Mormon period). Monumental construction and stelae characterize the Classic Mayan period that followed, as city-states formed throughout Central America. There were other rival civilizations present, including Teotihuacan, Tikal, and Calakmul. The Classic Mayan period dissolved in wars and environmental catastrophe by the 9th Century CE. These Classic Maya events post-date the Book of Mormon period, of course, and archeology tells us relatively little about what preceded them (Abrams, 1994; Coe, 1999).

Central America, in the absence of human construction, is typically dense jungle. It is also extremely active tectonically, and earthquakes and volcanic eruptions have forced the evacuation and rebuilding (usually in a different place) of numerous Spanish-era cities multiple times. These circumstances are not conducive to the preservation of any archeological artifacts except stone, and only if the stone is not buried by tens of meters of volcanic tephra.

The Book of Mormon itself says that, until the very end, the Nephite population was quite small, consistently numbering far fewer than surrounding hostile Lamanite populations. The Nephites and the Lamanites could communicate with each other, implying that the former was a related language subset of the latter; they apparently evolved over time in parallel, sharing elements back and forth (Stubbs, 2016). So... can you prove the Book of Mormon events, at least the ones in the New World, actually took place? Because of the tropical vegetation and tectonic environment, as we noted, it is virtually impossible to do this. In epistemology, the burden of proof (sometimes called onus probandi) is the obligation on a party in a dispute to provide sufficient information to support their position. *A negative proof is not a valid way to proceed.*

We can thank philosophy for this, by the way.

It is significant (and also probably not surprising) that the Middle Eastern component of the Book of Mormon has at least as much verification through archaeology, acquired only in the past several decades, as the Bible has received in the past several centuries. Historicity works moderately well in the eastern Mediterranean environment. Historicity is generally NOT really possible in a jungle environment frequently reshaped by massive volcanism.

Newer research in Central America is beginning to show interesting correlations with Book of Mormon events, however. For example, see John Sorenson's "Digging into the Book of Mormon" (https://www.lds.org/ensign/1984/09/digging-into-the-book-of-mormon-our-changing-understanding-of-ancient-america-and-its-scripture?lang=eng). Western North American and Central American Uto-Aztecan language and fossil linguistic structures have been recently and convincingly linked to Central and South Arabian Semitic languages (Stubbs, 2016). There is even a perhaps surprising explanation for this in the Book of Mormon itself (Alma 63: 4-9). Finally, one truly catastrophic event in the Book of Mormon (3 Nephi 8) can easily be explained by modern Central American geology (Kutterolf et al., 2008).

Nicaea

If you don't know about Nicaea, you cannot argue about *anything* religious.

Mark Twain is supposed to have said, "History doesn't repeat itself – but it sure does rhyme," so it is incumbent upon all of us to at least be aware of what has happened in the past, because it's the root of our present. How ironic and telling then to use this quote in this context, because it's really not clear that Twain even wrote or said it. (http://quoteinvestigator.com/2014/01/12/history-rhymes/).

Like this famous quote, however, there are many people who follow a faith-based tradition who don't really understand where that faith evolved from, nor do they realize who decided what they now believe in. Some faiths have even been condemned for not following "the Christian tradition." Evaluating this faulty accusation of not "being Christian" requires an understanding of history.

Several decades ago I was in Jordan to supervise a $2.5 million airborne geophysical survey. While there I was invited to an embassy dinner in Amman, where I encountered my first Catholic priest in quite a long time. Father Fulco was a Jesuit priest who by his own admission was an agnostic. He was a professor of archeology at Berkeley, specializing in ancient coinage. We hit it off – we had Berkeley and archeology and the same irreverent sense of humor in common, and he had a pungently expressed dislike of the Israelis who occupied the West Bank at the time (they returned the dislike with frosting).

After a while Father Fulco and I got onto religious topics, and the first time I saw him get serious was when he told me that as a member of the Church of Jesus Christ of Latter-Day Saints (he called me a "Mormon"), *that I was an "Arian,"* and therefore my baptism didn't count in an era where the Catholic church was beginning to accept protestant churches' baptisms. When I grew up, the Catholic nuns who taught me referred to the "Arian Heresy" as a Really Bad Thing. This sort of accusation (or dismissal of my faith) by Father Fulco didn't really throw a damper on our conversation – I was (and remain) less than uninterested in Catholic baptism. But it caused me to think about what turns out to be a major turning point – if not THE major turning point – in the early Christian church, the Great Apostacy. This is an idea that there had been a great falling away in the early centuries of the Christian church, as Paul had prophesied (2 Thessalonians

2:3-4). The name "Great Apostasy" stems from at least the Reformation and Luther (Talmage, 1909, reprinted 2014; Renan, 1890; Reu, 1944, among many others).

I was interested in using my free weekend. I had nothing to do that weekend except wait for contractor bids to arrive. Because there were no communication links between Jordan and Israel at the time – they were technically at war – I couldn't easily get to Jerusalem, nor make reservations ahead of time. Father Fulco gave me abundant excellent advice on how to get to Jerusalem ("take the absolute bare minimum, no more than a briefcase," and "be prepared for the closest 'feely' search of your life"). He also told me how to negotiate a room for several nights in the White Sisters Convent in Jerusalem after I got there. He told me to beg and grovel and insist on talking with the Mother Superior, who he said always caved in because she had such a kind heart. This gave me my one opportunity to spend several days in and around Jerusalem, the Temple Mount, and – especially – the Garden Tomb. The price I paid was $5/night – and being chewed to pieces by mosquitoes all night long, as I looked from my bed, unable to sleep, through a windowless hole in the wall upon the floodlight-lit walls of the Old City.

During those two long sleepless nights, I thought about Father Fulco's Arian accusation. In fact, members of the Church are *not* Arians, so bear with me here as I explain. Arius was one of several bishops in the 4th Century Christian church in Alexandria, Egypt, but to explain more fully, we need to give you some flavor first.

In 325 AD, the Roman emperor Constantine convened a gathering of Christian bishops at Nicaea in what is now thought to be northern Turkey (MacMullen, 1984; Brown, 2003). There were altogether too many different flavors of the "Christian" religion – especially beliefs in the Godhead – by that point in history. The arguments were particularly full of anger over the nature of Christ – and they were *furious* arguments. In fact, Constantine was not even a Christian at the time – he was only sprinkled with water on his death-bed twelve years later. Nevertheless, Constantine had made Christianity the state religion for political purposes, and things were not going swimmingly – so he demanded a consensus. What ensued was a classic example of the philosophies of men mingled with scripture. What the Emperor wants, of course, the Emperor gets. He didn't particularly care what that consensus was, as he was largely uninformed about Christianity, even though he had made it the official faith of the Roman Empire for strategic reasons.

The arguments at Nicaea went on for over two months, mainly

between three bishops named Arius, Saint Alexander of Alexandria, and Saint Athanasius (initially Alexander's personal secretary). These were all bishops at one time or another of the great Roman city of Alexandria. By their titles in the modern Catholic Church – "Saint" – you can guess who won: saints are supposed to be the good guys.

Arius claimed that the Son of God was a creation, made from nothing, that he was the first "thing" that God had created before time began; and that everything else was subsequently created through the Son. Arius also held that Christ was capable of His own free will of right and wrong, could make mistakes, and was a finite being. (If you know anything about Church of Jesus Christ theology, you'll see immediately why we are NOT Arians.)

Athanasius, on the other hand, held that God the Father and Christ were co-equal, had always existed together, and that Christ could not err. Despite getting to fisticuffs (Nicholas of Myra, later canonized as a saint, at one point slapped Arius in the face), a compromise was reached. Constantine stepped in at that point and forced upon the rest of the church the dogma now known as the Nicaean Creed. This included a declaration that the Father and the Son are of the same substance and are co-eternal, basing the declaration on the claim that *this was a formulation of traditional Christian belief handed down from the Apostles.* It wasn't, of course. The name of Athanasius is attached to this doxology.

Arius and a few devoted followers were excommunicated, exiled to Illyria, and their books were burned. Anyone found possessing Arian books somehow missed and not burned *was to be executed,* by order of Constantine. What the Emperor wants, the Emperor gets (Barnes, 1981; Ayers, 2006). Interestingly, no one today knows exactly where Nicaea actually was located, other than somewhere in the northwest of modern Turkey.

I reassured Father Fulco that no, I was NOT part of *"The Arian Heresy,"* as the nuns called it. Close, but no balloons – both the New Testament and modern Church of Jesus Christ revelation both give quite a different picture of the relationship of Christ to our Father in Heaven. Someone other than Christ was talking to John and Christ as they came out of the waters of baptism in the River Jordan, and someone other than God and Christ appeared in the form of a dove – in other words, three distinct and separate entities in the Godhead were present and distinct at Christ's baptism (Mark 1:9-11). Arius had gotten part of the way back through all the Gnostic philosophy add-ons over the previous two centuries, but he still missed this key point.

Can you distinguish what is taught by the Nicaean Creed and

subsequent religious policy and doctrinal convocations, from what you personally believe? Catholic dogma, and subsequent break-offs, including Maronite, Syriac, Greek Orthodox, Russian Orthodox, and Coptic churches, and then a millennium later Protestantism, have evolved further since Nicaea. You may wish to explore these evolutionary changes... they are interesting, to say the least. Even more interesting: to learn about the personalities, philosophies of men mingled with scripture, and even political strategies behind those various changes.

This exploration may lead you to reconsider what you personally believe. Then we recommend that you read the New Testament – read it again, if you already have – and this time draw your own conclusions about the nature of the Godhead *from the New Testament.* Subtract out the political history and Gnostic philosophy, and you will end up with something very simple and straightforward. We think you may prefer this.

Flavors of Philosophy

There is a bad version of everything. Diet Coke comes to mind.

We've mostly been correlating science and religion, and outlining the boundaries of each, but philosophy is important, too. In fact, modern science is intimately rooted in philosophy – in fact, what we call science was usually called natural philosophy in the 19th Century. From the time of Sophocles, Plato, and Aristotle, philosophy was humanity's attempt to understand the world around us, absent all but the most primitive forms of scientific experimentation and testing (direct evidence accessible to the human eye). Much of the history of philosophy during the past millennium, however, is distracting. It reads more like a cycle of Young Turks creating dense formulations revisiting the reigning philosophies of that day – then being undercut by each succeeding generation of philosophers, intent on being the Next New Thing. If you search for lists of branches of philosophy, you will find a list of five, a list of six, a list of seven, a list of ten... but you won't see existentialism pop up. Sartre and Camus are already outdated. In the meantime, experimental science gathered itself into a real head of steam that finally began to explode in the 19th Century.

While philosophy like science is evolutionary, there are elements of it that stick – that are critically important. In part this is because there are a lot of persistent kinds of philosophy:
- Logic (probably best described as the study of the most effective way to think),
- Epistemology (reason vs. revelation, the nature and limits of human knowledge),
- Ethics (moral principles, rules of conduct),
- Political philosophy (democracy is a mess, but consider the alternatives),
- Philosophy of language (why did you say that... in that particular way?), and
- Philosophy of science (how does one actually *do* rigorous science?).

We deliberately left out things like existentialism, meta-philosophies like the multiverse, nihilism, fruitcakes, and toasters, although most people still take toasters fairly seriously.

It could in fact be argued that science owes its modern success to philosophy, that ideas evolving from Kant to Hegel to Popper about reality, hypothesis, and falsifiability gave modern science a guiding framework to work within. Good science requires good, logical thinking, and philosophy is where it all began.

Our smartphones, which are more capable than the desk-size computer that we learned to program FORTRAN and C++ on, are a metaphor for the accelerating advance of science and technology. Rapid and accelerating technological advances can also fool otherwise smart people. Some scientists are so entranced with scientific progress and technology (they sometimes conflate these two) that they have made the unjustifiable assumption that science has supplanted religion as well. They implicitly and sometimes even explicitly believe that modern science is the pinnacle, or final and complete truth. This is called scientism (see our earlier chapter with that name). This particular self-anointing conceit would *appear* to be fairly common if you listen only to the loudest voices... among scientists in good health. We have observed that rather few scientists who belong to a faith tradition are inclined to get in other people's faces about it. Dismissing religion and calling modern science the final and complete truth, however, is also circular logic, and displays a profound ignorance of the history of science.

In the last century the boundaries of science, religion, and philosophy seem to have blurred, but a careless acceptance that this is okay or normal would be a big mistake. *Philosophy can only speculate about the truly Big Questions*, such as:

- Why did the universe begin 13.8 billion years ago?
- Where did *I* come from?
- *Why* am I *here – and why can I even think about this?*
- What will happen to me after my liver/kidneys/brain fall apart?

...but philosophy can never *answer* these questions. Why? Because philosophy operates without the irritating constraint of data. At the same time, science cannot answer those fundamental questions either – because it also cannot *access* the relevant data. Cosmic microwave background radiation and observed evidence of human evolution are very limited and extremely fragmentary.

Stephen Jay Gould argued that science and religion are different "non-overlapping magisteria" (Gould, 1997) – e.g., independent domains that seek to answer different questions by totally different means.

This, however, deliberately side-steps the fragmentary data issue and creates an artificial barrier, because science and religion are both seeking the same larger truth. They are just using different means to get to the same place. Like the philosophers of old, if you don't have data, you are not constrained in what you may propose, *but neither are the rest of us constrained to accept your opinions.* We see growing evidence instead that ultimately all truth (as opposed to the philosophical or scientific conceit du jour) goes back to just one thing: The Source of Everything. If the universe started with a Big Bang 13.8 billion years ago, then *something preceded it. It didn't just happen. There is causality in everything we look at.*

> "*All religions, arts and sciences are branches of the same tree.*"
> – Albert Einstein, letter to Sigmund Freud, 30 July 1932.

Faust

Making another bet on God – and not a good one.

Wolfgang Goethe spent 25 years perfecting his two-part play "Faustus," completing it in 1832, the year he died (Goethe, 1832; Phillips, 1911). It is considered the greatest work of German literature, perhaps of ALL literature, and is both haunting and mesmerizing. It is so complex that we won't even attempt to outline it here. At its core is a man who, in seeking ever greater knowledge, makes a bargain with the Devil to get it. In return for granting everything he wants and seeks, Faust must sign over his soul. The story has a bittersweet ending, with unselfish love a key element. Faust was bored, feeling trapped and limited. He did not seek power through this knowledge, but instead he wanted access to transcendent knowledge unavailable from the science and the wisdom of his age.

Over the years, many have interpreted this bargain as one that a lot of people make: to take great risks to live an exciting life, to potentially sacrifice everything to get wealthy or to avoid being bored. In our modern culture this is part of what is now called the *Faustian Bargain*. It is an idea that predates Goethe and is widespread in Western culture, found in many fairy tales with a typical slant: a warning lesson.

There's an old saying, "There ain't no such thing as a free lunch." You could condense all the conservation laws of physics into these nine words, because nothing comes without a cost. Chemical reaction equations must balance. One plus one must equal two. $E = mc^2$.

Many of us may have wondered if we have somehow ourselves made a Faustian bargain – especially when we seek wider experience, greater knowledge. Were the permanent health consequences of enthralling jungle trips, the deadly risks of harrowing desert expeditions, really worth it? For those who have experimented with drugs, the consequences are often more immediate – and more devastating.

There's a larger lesson here. We're not sure we would trade any of our experiences away in retrospect, but we also wonder: if we knew *ahead of time* what the long-range price would be, how close one of us would come to death, would he still board that helicopter into the jungle each time? Climb into that Hummer and start that 1,700 kilometer-long, open desert crossing? Assume we could just *walk* out of Mount St Helens crater?

However, isn't that what life is all about? We make choices, and there is always a price affixed to each one. We may not see that price, and we may not *want* to see that price. A good friend wanted to know if the guy proposing marriage to her was The One – but was afraid of the answer she would get if she prayed for divine guidance. So, she just married him. She's divorced now. My father, my grandfather, and my great-grandfather each made awful choices that left their wives alone and their children fatherless. They *each* ended their long lives sad and lonely.

We cringe when we see someone make a family-changing decision like a quickie marriage, or a divorce, or an affair – and commonly they deliberately choose *not* to consider the long-term consequences. We don't *need* to seek out adventure; it generally finds us anyway.

The measure of wisdom is to always weigh the downrange consequences before we board that exciting helicopter. Weigh that Faustian bargain carefully before you sign with your blood... because the consequences always last longer than the reward up front, just like that last car-loan.

Also keep in mind that **wisdom correlates rather poorly with either IQ or education**, so don't trust your emotions OR your brains, but ask the wiser people around you. You know who they are.

Then *listen.*

The Color of the Door

Have you thought much about when you check out of this hotel?

That's really a metaphor for dying.

Nature magazine had an article about how 13,000 years ago humans began to domesticate plants – which made it possible to live longer (Diamond, 2002). The crucial down-range consequence: grandparents, with all the cultural survival memories (and increased survival for the grandchildren) that this development led to.

Science leads us back to families again.

Two articles in an issue of Scientific American discuss (a) the evolution of grandparents (Caspari, 2011) and (b) the multiverse concept: this second is the idea that we live in just one of an *infinite* number of universes, and this particular universe just happens to have the physical constants all perfectly aligned to support life (Ellis, 2011). Given enough time – and enough food – mankind can come up with a lot of great ideas. Art. Science. Ways for me to waste time playing electronic games. In a previous section, we pointed out that concepts like a multiverse – and for that matter string theory – are absolutely unprovable. The Ellis article took the time to actually point out *why* they are both unprovable: they are concepts, ideas, but neither are even *remotely* testable theories. Worse, they start and end with circular logic. A *scientific* theory is a fully-developed and self-consistent concept that is also consistent with observed physical facts. It already works with some existing data and just needs to be tested and refined to deal with ALL data.

Ideas (concepts/philosophies) go beyond a theory when, like evolution or relativity, they can be shown to explain things that haven't yet been reported, to predict something into the future that can then be verified. Thus, the theory of evolution isn't really a theory anymore – it's just evolution. It has been repeatedly tested at widely different scales of size and time and found to be consistent with observed facts. We've personally witnessed the immediate results of natural selection in Venezuela (rats than can climb up vertical steel bars), as well as in mice left by a Spanish ship anchored in southeast Alaska over 400 years ago. The latter led to two harrowing nights for us in a Forest Service cabin on San Fernando Island, trying to deal with the Black Fluff-Balls from Hell that could jump a meter high, trying to get into our food. Evolution doesn't *threaten* our faith, it *augments* it. It's one of His most elegant tools. We talk about this in greater detail in two previous chapters.

So why worry about these sorts of things at all? Our ancestors thousands of years ago didn't have the luxury to worry because they were too busy farming or hunting down the next meal. We, however, have the luxury of thinking about these things because we have plenty of food and comfortable housing – in large part because of science (or actually engineering and technology). Unfortunately, a majority of our brothers and sisters in the United States (and a supermajority beyond its frontiers) do not have the luxury of good housing and secure food supplies. They struggle to pay their mortgages, and in many cases struggle just to put food on the table for their children.

And to what end do they struggle so?

Well, perhaps they love their children and don't want to feed them stones. (*"Or what man is there of you, whom if his son ask bread, will he give him a stone?"* – Mathew 7:9)

And for the non-believing scientists out there who have the luxury of reading Scientific American, Science, Nature, and Discover magazines? To what end do they "do science"?

It's fun, for sure. However, we suspect that some want to think that they are more important than a temporary blip on a cosmic wave-function. They don't want to admit their mortality: to admit that they will die and be forgotten with time. To admit that they aren't important to anyone. *Not even a little bit, if this is all they can do for others while on the earth.*

We didn't forget about the title above, so, now to answer this: the color of *what* door? That's a metaphor that one of us (Jeff) started using many years ago. A dear friend of ours died in Tucson, Arizona, when Jeff was 26 and the friend was 30. Another friend we both grew to know and admire at the Cascades Volcano Observatory was a master photographer on the side, and his life work had quite a number of photographs of doors from all over the world. Each door seemed to be a different color, to have its own unique character. Each door is different – has a different color in the metaphor – because each one leads to a different place for each individual on this planet: how you will die, and exactly where you will go is unique to you above all other human beings who have ever lived. Each door is different.

Like each of us.

Buck, our friend in Tucson, died of a raging autoimmune disease – manifested as blindness resulting from diabetes, which eventually destroyed his kidneys and other organs. Dave, our friend at the Cascades Volcano Observatory, survived a horrific multi-year experience in Vietnam. However, he did not survive exposure to Agent Orange, and died of the most virulent of the four known versions of thyroid cancer. Both of these friends started out as very ordinary people but ended their lives as what we would call extraordinary, even great, people: They had reconciled themselves with who they were in this great universe. They had gotten to the point in life when *the most important things they did were what they could do for other people. They were living that kind of life – a Christ-like life – when they departed this world.*

That's what is important. *Not* the brand of our shoes or the existence of a multiverse.

So. What will be the color of OUR door? Will we depart via lung cancer? It took Jeff's Dad and his grandmother, but he has avoided tobacco since he was 20. A stroke perhaps? It took Jeff's Mom and *her* Dad, but Jeff has exercised and eaten carefully since he was in his 30's.

One thing for sure: our door *will* have a color – it will be distinctive and unique to each of us. As Jim Morrison of The Doors once said (the title of his autobiography) *"No one gets out of here alive"* (Morrison, 1980).

Morrison also said, "People fear death even more than pain. It's strange that they fear death. Life hurts a lot more than death. At the point of death, the pain is over. Yeah, I guess it is a friend."

As scientists, we're moderately interested in what the color of our doors will be, but we're much more interested in having time to leave messages of love for the kids and grandkids we care about so much. Ultimately, they must follow a similar path, and then depart this life by themselves. This is, after all, why we're writing this book. We both actually look forward to stepping through that door and finally going home – ultimately, to be together forever.

As Anchises said to Aeneas when he visited him in the Underworld:

> *"At last! Are you here at last?*
> *I always trusted that your sense of right*
> *Would prevail and keep you going to the end.*
> *And am I now allowed to see your face,*
> *My son, and hear you talk, and talk to you myself?*
>
> *This is what I imagined and looked forward to*
> *As I counted the days; and my trust was not misplaced.*
> *To think of the lands and the outlying seas*
> *You have crossed, my son, to receive this welcome..."*

(Virgil, The Aeneid Book VI: A New Verse Translation, Book VI, translator Seamus Heaney)

Victor's History, Skewed History, False History

I won the battle of Kadesh. I can *prove* it.

Historians and scientists are not all that different. Both deal with assessing conflicting data, both require balancing information with hard facts – when available. Now, this is older than old to professional historians out there, but it's true that history is written by the victors. We might add that it is also written by those with an agenda. Truth is rather often *not* the truth in verbal form, and often not the truth even in the written form, or at least not the complete truth. It's simply the opinion of the most articulate (and/or loudest) person on the block, and they ALL have an agenda. That's close to saying that all truth is subjective – but not quite.

Pearl Harbor and the Bataan Death-March were held up to us as children in school as examples of Japanese war-time evil and perfidy. The Allies were the Good Guys, the saviors of civilization. However, we never heard much about the fire-bombing of Tokyo, where upwards of 100,000 men, women, and children died (Long, Tony [March 9, 2011], "March 9, 1945: Burning the Heart Out of the Enemy": Wired Magazine. Retrieved June 22, 2018). Moreover, one of our uncles, as a German prisoner of war, was a personal witness to the horrific Dresden fire-bombing of February 1945. Virtually all of the victims were civilians, deliberately massacred by the Allies to demoralize a combatant nation. *That* was not discussed in our college history classes either (de Bruhl, 2006).

Ramses the Great (Ramses II) lost the battle of Kadesh-Barnea around 1,250 BC. He lost it badly. Hittite forces cleverly baited him, and he led the Egyptian army into attacking a small Hittite force, thereby exposing him and his strung-out army to a devastating ambush. Ramses suffered a tactical and strategic defeat that he barely survived; he did so only by abandoning his personal Ra Division troops to the mercies of the Hittites. You would never know this from the victory monuments that Ramses later erected in Egypt, however. According to those monuments, Ramses was the great victor, the savior of Egyptian civilization from the bearded barbarians, the father of over 100 children – and the one who wrote his version of history into monumental stone (Grimal, 1992).

The Protocols of the Elders of Zion is another example of fake history – alternative facts. This hideous document has been proven repeatedly to be fraudulent – a clumsy anti-Semitic propaganda effort put to rest, and then later resurrected and propagated by Nazi Germany. With each new generation of anti-Semites, this thing has taken on a Phoenix-like life of its own. As Josef Goebbels, Hitler's propaganda chief famously said, "*If you tell a lie big enough and keep repeating it, people will eventually come to believe it*" (Goebbels, 1941).

Depending on who you listen to, Joseph Smith elaborated on some local Indian legends and wrote a very imaginative novel – or he actually did translate a block of golden, minutely-inscribed plates seen and hefted by at least 12 people. They recorded their impressions in two published affidavits and numerous personal journals.

Which version of history is correct?

From painful experience, we automatically tend to discount anything written by prominent headline-grabbing detractors of religion, as they have a transparent agenda – and have shown no qualms about dredging up old accusations against the Church of Jesus Christ, its founder, and the Book of Mormon, accusations which we know from personal experience have long since been disproven. Other statements these individuals have each written about other people and other issues are contested by (even atheist) scholars as dishonest or incompetent at best, fraudulent at worst, so why should anyone believe anything *any* religion-haters write about *anything*?

Which leads us to this question: what history can you trust?

As evidence-driven scientists we've thought a lot about this. We have concluded, like most historians, that only something we could see supporting evidence for (first or second hand) might be considered reasonably reliable. Uncle James's account of the bombing of Dresden is reliable: we know him personally to be an individual of very high personal integrity... *and he was there. He watched it unfold.*

What about supportive evidence for Joseph Smith? Journals of individuals who viewed the Golden Plates describe leafing through the individual pages; at least two journals describe the 20 cm (8-inch) cubed block of plates as weighing roughly ~27 kg (60 lbs (Doxey, 1986; De Groote, 2010). With slight variations the journal entries all agree on most details, not unlike the four Gospels. Besides never recanting their affidavits, there is another ancillary piece of logic we could apply. Could *you* get 11 people to sign affidavits that they saw and held gold plates – and never recant those statements – from a two-kilometer radius around *your* home?

Utah holds the US record for the most advanced degrees per capita, and Church of Jesus Christ members are responsible for the lion's share of these. The conclusion is obvious: Church members do not fear the truth, wherever it may be found. In fact, Church leaders actively encourage advanced education, something inconsistent with a premise based on lies and deceit.

We've also considered our own personal experiences. As scientists, we have gathered in personal journals a rather long series of small but cumulative pieces of evidence that ALL tell us that we're not following a lie. In these journals we have recorded consistent answers to prayers, amazing results from blessings, and even what we're bold enough to call personal revelation. These have consistently withstood testing and have been verified with time. When we want answers to specific things not clear in Church history (or seek direction in our own scientific research efforts), *we know that we can always get the answers.* Sometimes they arrive many years after we began searching. But they always arrive.

There are other things that are somewhat harder to document, such as the strong internal conceptual self-consistency and the utterly pragmatic doctrinal-philosophical framework underlying our faith. We are constantly astounded at the ability of this doctrine to explain personally-observed life experiences.

This personal approach to gathering the truth about events nearly 200 years old in Church history is not unlike the methods we use in our professional research science. We gather evidence – almost all of it *indirect* evidence. As with our scientific research, our approach to these spiritual matters is falsifiable – it is *testable*. Personal revelation has checked out for us individually and together, sooner or later, 100 percent of the time.

Years ago, we had a friend in Virginia who was troubled by certain anti-LDS writings. There seems to be a small sub-culture of people who accumulate and publish these sorts of things. Of course, this makes little sense – for instance why would they even care? But Mike would bring one to our attention and challenge us. One of us would dutifully research the issue, and it was always something *said* by one person, and always third- or fourth-hand in nature. There *were* some shameful events in Church history – the Mountain Meadows Massacre, for instance. However, in the vast majority of the instances Mike referred us to, we always were able to satisfy ourselves that someone (for whatever suspect personal agenda) was simply out to cause damage, creating from whole cloth their own version of the Protocols of the Elders of Zion.

After a while, we realized that our debunking efforts were a huge waste of time. We concluded that the cumulative evidence that we can see, particularly but not exclusively in our own lives, vastly outweighs the negatives that Mike and others might dump on us. We realized that we need not bother anymore to even pursue these ugly things – we're too busy cataloging our own supportive personal experiences in our journals. All these things we know first-hand, and they convince us that we are on the right path.

> *"Brothers and sisters, this is a divine work in process, with the manifestations and blessings of it abounding in every direction, so please don't hyperventilate if from time to time issues arise that need to be examined, understood, and resolved. They do and they will. In this Church, what we know will always trump what we do not know. And remember, in this world, everyone is to walk by faith.... So be kind regarding human frailty—your own as well as that of those who serve with you in a Church led by volunteer, mortal men and women. Except in the case of His only perfect Begotten Son, imperfect people are all God has ever had to work with. That must be terribly frustrating to Him, but He deals with it. So should we. And when you see imperfection, remember that the limitation is not in the divinity of the work. I know that Joseph Smith, who acknowledged that he wasn't perfect, was nevertheless the chosen instrument in God's hand to restore the everlasting gospel to the earth. "*
> –Jeffrey R. Holland, April 2013 General Conference.

Joseph Smith readily admitted to being imperfect, just like Moses did, like Peter did, and like Paul did. Only Christ and The Father are perfect.

One final thing to consider: At the time Joseph Smith was murdered in 1844, the population of Nauvoo was roughly 12,000 souls, rivaling the population of Chicago at the time. In the terrible confusion and sadness that followed Joseph's death, Brigham Young took charge as the presiding authority – the president of the Quorum of the Twelve Apostles. In the bitter winter of 1846-47 virtually the entire Church population in and around Nauvoo, Illinois, decamped for Iowa. There they lived in frozen misery for several months, then they moved westward in a long and dangerous overland trek to the Great Salt Lake Basin to re-establish their new Zion. Everyone in that population knew everything that had gone on with Joseph Smith – gossip in any community moves quickly. If their prophet had been doing bad things, everyone would have known about it. Yet some 12,000 people gave up their comfortable, warm homes and marched into the cold, dangerous, largely unknown western wilderness together.

We consider this the strongest vote one could possibly make about the character of Joseph Smith, and the door to the truth that he opened with the Restoration. Twelve thousand people *voted with their feet* – *12,000 people who all personally knew Joseph Smith.* That simple historical fact speaks volumes, and it's documented in hundreds of personal journals and historical records.

We are satisfied that we've found the truth and are happy to follow it. Our goal now is to hold onto the iron rod and endure to the end.

After all, Christ said, *"Come, follow me."*

That's really not so hard to do.

...And Deliberately One-Eyed History

Put on this blindfold. You can trust us. *Sure* you can.

We begin with an anecdote:

Many of us during our lifetimes will have to wear an eye-patch. We may have amblyopia ("wandering eye") as a child, or we may have an infection, or we may scratch the cornea by rubbing the eye when sand gets into it. There may be an injury, temporary or permanent. Whenever we wear an eye patch, we have something called mono-vision. We no longer have stereo vision, and our depth perception is seriously impaired. We may stumble over a sidewalk edge, we may walk into a door jamb. We are visually crippled, and we have continuing problems from our one-eyed vision.

Why do we mention this? Consider the following.

In science we must evaluate data that we collect, and there are arguments on how we do this. As we write this there are at least two major schools of how to use statistics in science: how to calculate a numerical probability, from a given set of data, that a certain answer or conclusion is true. The main schools of thought are called Bayesian and Fisherian. The former school teaches that a prior understanding – keeping an eye on what we think are the physical processes involved – must be built into the calculation, and there is a deceptively simple equation to do that [$P(H|E) = P(E|H)P(E)P(H)$]. (For *much* more on this, including those probability variables, see Silver, 2012). Implicit in this approach is that we are thinking about the larger picture – the underlying principles. The Fisherian statistical school, which still dominates the biology field at this time, believes that all information is contained only in the dataset. To a Fisherian statistics person, a prior understanding is only a bias, and must be discounted, or it's not good science.

However, any scientist who has collected data knows that there are data and there is noise: random noise, systemic noise, and measurement noise. The tendency to evaluate all the data blindly means that in many cases we are trying to fit a solution to noise. In simplest terms, this is trying to draw a curve through dots scattered all over a graph. A least-squares fit line to some data points is called a regression fit, or just a regression. If there is significant noise, this line can tilt in a number of different directions depending on how the points are "weighted" – how important the scientist thinks the outliers are. In simplest terms, we are trying to make sense out of junk. This leads as you can imagine to study after study that contradicts other earlier studies on the same topic. One has only to read the popular science magazines or the morning news to become painfully aware that "science" disagrees with itself at least as often as it agrees. Does coffee contribute to heart attacks or longer life? The answer depends profoundly on how you analyze the data – and how large a dataset you have, and how many variables are involved. In the media we have seen both results given as if a final conclusion has been reached. One newspaper reports that *"Four cups of coffee a day linked to improved heart health, study finds"* (Hosie, 2018). But read the original scientific article and you might wonder where in the world that conclusion came from (Ale-Agha, 2018). Now read American Heart Association (2014). What do you believe now?

Regression analysis

FITS A STRAIGHT LINE TO THIS MESSY SCATTERPLOT. x IS CALLED THE INDEPENDENT OR PREDICTOR VARIABLE, AND y IS THE DEPENDENT OR RESPONSE VARIABLE. THE REGRESSION OR PREDICTION LINE HAS THE FORM

$$y = a+bx$$

Figure 3. Regression Analysis (from madhureshkumar.wordpress.com).

Figure 3 gives you a sense of how this kind of data analysis exercise can lead to many different possible interpretations, or conclusions. So, what or who can you believe? A talk given by Jeffrey R. Holland or the Quorum of Twelve Apostles titled "Lord, I Believe" (April 2013 General Conference) is remarkably insightful. He points out that there are people who, despite even spending a lifetime in the Church, will find some small item that really upsets them. In other words, a single point out away from the best-fit regression curve draws their focused attention. They may not understand why polygamy took place, they may not understand why the Mountain Meadows Massacre took place, they are bothered by something that a Church leader (Relief Society President, Bishop, General Authority, President of the Church) has said.

I could once count myself in this group. A Church family in our former neighborhood instructed their eight children to attack our 7-year-old son whenever they encountered him playing in our neighborhood cul-de-sac. They later acknowledged that on further investigation they realized that our son had actually NOT struck their 3-year-old daughter, but by that time the damage was done, and there was anger on both sides. The idea of encountering that couple in the hallways of our chapel led me to suggest to my wife, who had taken the brunt of the social ostracism, that we simply stop attending church. I will never forget her response.

"Last I checked, this was CHRIST'S church, not XXX's church!"

Again: Are we looking at the tree, or the forest?

Elder Holland's key point is this: hang onto the things you KNOW. Do *not* be afraid to seek answers for something that bothers you, but *don't throw everything else out for one or two negative things that bother or offend you.* In his words:

> *"Now, with the advantage that nearly 60 years give me since I was a newly believing 14-year-old, I declare some things I now know. I know that God is at all times and in all ways and in all circumstances our loving, forgiving Father in Heaven. I know Jesus was His only perfect child, whose life was given lovingly by the will of both the Father and the Son for the redemption of all the rest of us who are not perfect. I know He rose from that death to live again, and because He did, you and I will also. I know that Joseph Smith, who acknowledged that he wasn't perfect, was nevertheless the chosen instrument in God's hand to restore the everlasting gospel to the earth. I also know that in doing so—particularly through translating the Book of Mormon—he has taught me more of God's love, of Christ's divinity, and of priesthood power than any other prophet of whom I have ever read, known, or heard in a lifetime of seeking. I know that President Thomas S. Monson, who moves devotedly and buoyantly toward the 50th anniversary of his ordination as an Apostle, is the rightful successor to that prophetic mantle today. We have seen that mantle upon him again in this conference. I know that 14 other men whom you sustain as prophets, seers, and revelators sustain him with their hands, their hearts, and their own apostolic keys."*—Jeffrey R. Holland, April 2013 Ensign, p. 96.

I remember uncounted priesthood blessings that suddenly healed me, or in once case brought a man out of a four-day coma (he sat bolt upright in his hospital bed as I laid my hands on his head and called his name in order to give him a blessing). I still keep the list of the 13 steps that all had to happen *in sequence* for our family to move to Venezuela, where incredible adventures and opportunities awaited all of us. A failure to complete just one of the complicated steps would have aborted the entire three-year stay. It was equivalent to thirteen coin-flips all ending up heads. A few of these events and blessings would have been remarkable coincidences, but the aggregate of them all is immense – and compelling.

Our advice: DON'T get all wrapped up in a single tree. Look at the entire forest. If you feel your faith is being shaken by something, first *consider who benefits from this?* Then remember this from Elder Holland's talk:

> "When doubt or difficulty come, do not be afraid to ask for help. If we want it as humbly and honestly as this father [see Mark 9:22–24; also verses 14–21] did, we can get it. The scriptures phrase such earnest desire as being of "real intent," pursued "with full purpose of heart, acting no hypocrisy and no deception before God.[verse 11]" We testify that in response to that kind of importuning, God will send help *from both sides of the veil* to strengthen our belief." –ibid (emphasis ours).

This requires some patience, or a little faith, however you wish to view it.

But from our vantage point, it's soooo worth it.

Evidence, Critics, and Archaeology – What can we really prove?

Turns out almost nothing

Let's talk about evidence:

Archeologists have found ancient records inscribed on stones and on metal plates; can something like this be a means to "prove" the Book of Mormon? Graffiti in the geologically stable (and jungle-free) north Yemen makes it look like Nephi and his brothers were there. There are structures that look like baptismal fonts, temples, and altars in Central America. There are abundant writings and oral traditions about a white bearded god who appeared to the people in Central America and promised to come again. *An entire Aztec army bowed down when Hernán Cortés invaded the Valley of Mexico in 1521!* Many other elements seem to "prove" that the Book of Mormon is the accurate set of ancient documents that it claims to be. These are well documented in a number of books and articles listing these and many other features, including Nibley (1967), Hilton & Hilton (1976), Welch (1969), Sorensen (1985), Baer (1986), Ball (1993), Gee (1997), Kowallis (1999), Jordan (2003), and Stubbs (2016), among others.

And... more recent evidence:

Most recently, Brian Stubbs summarized in great detail the linguistic links between the probable Lehite languages of Aramaic, Hebrew, and Egyptian with modern Uto-Aztecan. This native American language group, recognized since the early 1900's, is found in western Central American and western North America, ranging from southern Oregon to Panama. Over 1,500 cognates and linguistic structures connect this language group with an ancient Semitic Arabian origin, and give remarkable new insights into the dispersion of the Nephite and the Mulekite groups in the western hemisphere. Awkward, un-English cognitive-accusative structures like "I dreamed a dream," and persistent use of the Hebrew possessive construct state such as "Sword of Laban" instead of "Laban's Sword" permeate the Book of Mormon. Church leadership has discouraged making more-readily-readable, modern English versions of the book because "...this process may introduce doctrinal errors or *obscure evidence of its ancient origin*" (Church Handbook 2, 21.1.8; *emphasis ours*).

Taken in whole these would seem pretty hard to argue against.

However, when confronted with such detail, even adding linguistic analytical evidence that the authors of the various books in the Book of Mormon were actually different people, and each used different words and grammatical structures... or that the language of the Book of Mormon is very different from the English language of 1830's New York ... or that the names and objects mentioned in the Book of Mormon are authentic and consistent with the languages and geography of the Frankincense Trail... or that the poetic forms in the Book of Mormon (chiasmus, etc.) are the same as those used in the Hebrew Old Testament...

Well, you will still always find critics who will not accept these as evidence of the book's veracity. Get used to it.

How *much* more evidence is necessary?

Even when confronted with affidavits of eleven witnesses who saw and "hefted" the plates, recording their experience in personal journals, critics then and now claim these people were lying or delusional. *All eleven of them? For the entire rest of their lives?* How about this: over 12,000 people, almost the entire resident population, left their homes in Nauvoo, Illinois, in the dead of the terrible 1846-47 winter, to head out into the unknown and very dangerous western wilderness. They could have stayed warm and safe – but it would have required disavowing their murdered prophet. Yet 12,000 people – *virtually all of whom personally knew Joseph Smith* – chose instead to march out into the frozen wastes of eastern Iowa, and then on to Nebraska, and eventually Utah.

They voted with their feet.

Despite overwhelming historical evidence such as this, the record shows that a small group of determined critics cannot accept the fact that these people knew Joseph Smith was a prophet, and they refused to deny their beliefs. What if at some point someone finds some ancient metal plates with characters just like those copied from the Book of Mormon plates, and when translating them, finds they say exactly what those characters are translated to say in the Book of Mormon? Or what if some researcher finds an ancient site in the jungle-and-volcanic-tephra-covered New World that somehow, miraculously, still preserves inscriptions just like those in the Book of Mormon, or finds some historical document that recounts one or more of the same histories told in the Book of Mormon?

Will determined cynics finally conclude that the Book of Mormon is therefore what it claims to be? Don't hold your breath – they won't.

There are four reasons for this:

1. Cynics will always have a response to every one of these pieces of evidence *in isolation*. For example, an anti-Church "outreach" group has come up with a number of objections to the idea that the three consonants on that altar in northern Yemen mean the same as the word "Nahom." As students of Arabic, we must say their arguments are wrong; as students of the Book of Mormon, we must say their arguments are misguided; and as students of human nature, we must say their arguments reveal a singular, determined mental self-blinding that undermines everything else they could possibly write. Scientists call this behavior "cherry-picking."

These people say, "Let us not forget that the Church has provided no historical or archaeological evidence that Nephi or any of the unique characters mentioned in the *Book of Mormon* actually lived." Of course, there is no archeological evidence that David or Solomon lived, either. Or even that the Huns used horses (Stubbs, 2016). *Really!*

2. To elaborate that point: There is absolutely no archaeological evidence of the Torah, of the sojourn in Egypt, of Moses, or of *any* of the patriarchs for that matter. There is no archaeological evidence whatsoever that Jericho was attacked by Hebrew-speaking tribesmen, nor even that there ever was a Hebrew invasion of Canaan. Let us not forget, either, that nobody has ever provided any archaeological evidence that the Council of Nicaea actually happened in 325 AD, and for that matter in the place in modern Turkey accepted for 1,600 years since it supposedly took place. Most Christian doxologies hinge on this one event, *but there is no archeological evidence that it ever took place.*

As Church of Jesus Christ writer John Gee notes,

"From historical sources we know that Nicaea was near Constantine's summer residence of Masuwari. We have no archaeological evidence that he was ever there or ever paid any attention to the place. The lack of archaeological evidence does not prove Constantine was never there. On the other hand, archaeological evidence tells us that the theater seated 15,000. I know of no historical evidence that provides us that information. The lack of historical evidence does not mean there was no theater" (Gee, 1997).

Gee also cites the difficulty of reconciling archaeological with historical evidence about the dynamic succession at Masuwari, concluding, "So we can only work with inadequate evidence." He concludes:

"Sometimes historical and archaeological evidence overlap. Sometimes they conflict. Most of the time they do neither. Each provides its own sort of evidence. One cannot just expect the two types of evidence to corroborate each other. Much of the material in the Bible, for example, is not and cannot be corroborated archaeologically. There are points at which the archaeological record does corroborate the Bible. But archaeology does not necessarily corroborate every point one might like" (Gee, 1997).

Another example is in the field of Mesoamerican studies, from Church writer William Hamblin, responding to yet another attack from an anti-Church of Jesus Christ writer who claims that the historical veracity of the Book of Mormon can't be proven from archaeological finds, so it must therefore not be true.

Hamblin writes about the names of known Mayan kings: "Only [a] dozen or two Maya personal names are attested in pre-400 AD inscriptions" (Hamblin, 2015). He lists these names and adds:

"Thus, from all of the New World, we have the names of twelve kings before 400 AD. That is a remarkably sparse database to work with. Basically, we have insufficient information from inscriptional archaeology to tell us anything substantial about Preclassic Mesoamerican history during the [Book of Mormon] period (which is precisely why it is called the Preclassic). There is plenty of archaeological evidence to demonstrate that there were many important cities and kingdoms in Preclassic times; we simply don't know the names of those cities or kings. Thus, again, the problem is not that the [Book of Mormon] somehow fails this test. The problem is that there is insufficient data to undertake that test. If we had for Preclassic Mesoamerica the amount of data we have for classical Greece, and there was no mention of plausible Nephites, that would be decisive evidence against the [Book of Mormon]. But since we lack that quantity and quality of evidence, the methodologically sound response is that the issue is unresolved."

Well, can we prove the Book of Mormon to be a historically accurate document based on current "inscriptional" archaeological knowledge? No, we cannot. Can we prove that it's NOT historically accurate by the same means? No, we cannot. This is just the reality of archeological data and historical records. Therefore, the people who argue against the

Book of Mormon based on lack of evidence are displaying startling ignorance of existing evidence and a basic science that they are invoking. There is also the philosophical and scientific fact that you cannot prove something does not exist just because you haven't seen it for yourself. *This is the Black Swan argument – a logical fallacy is so old that it has its own name: The Argument from Ignorance.*

3. Other Church scholars have noted the fact that the Nephites of the Book of Mormon were small in comparison to surrounding Pre-Classic Mayan populations (Sorenson, 1992), suggesting that they were unlikely to leave behind large mounds or artifacts for us to find.

Note that the book itself recounts huge disruptions in local topography (see 3 Nephi 8, for example). The Central American geologic record makes it rather stunningly clear that the topography is a living, evolving thing because of the high rate of tectonic plate subduction and its related volcanism. Spanish colonial records indicate that several cities in Central America were destroyed and abandoned, or moved, in historical times due to earthquakes and huge tephra falls changing the previous landscape. These include Guatemala City, obliterated in 1509 by a massive earthquake, then destroyed again and moved in 1773. San Salvador, the capital of El Salvador, was totally destroyed in 1625 and rebuilt on a nearby site. In 1610, Momotombo volcano erupted, destroying the capital of Nicaragua at the time. It was rebuilt as Managua, northwest of what is now known as the ruins of Old León. In 1854, San José, which was then the capital city of Costa Rica, was also completely destroyed. In 1902, Santa Maria volcano erupted with a force more than 10 times greater than Mount St Helens in 1980 – it was the third largest volcanic eruption in the world in the 20th Century. About 5.5 cubic kilometers of magma and tephra blown out by the eruption badly damaged the large nearby city of Quetzaltenango and buried the city of El Palmar, forcing the latter to be rebuilt elsewhere as Nuevo Palmar. It's therefore hard for us to understand why some people persist in speculating about where the geographical locations mentioned in the Book of Mormon might be.

4. It actually doesn't matter whether archaeological or historical evidence is found that supports the authenticity of the Bible or the Book of Mormon. If anything like that ever happens, it will be just another very localized ancient record. Scholars will be able to read it like they do the Dead Sea Scrolls (which themselves document only fragmentary evidence of a tiny community that survived barely a hundred years in relative isolation).

Readers will then marvel at the way the people lived back then, the struggles they had, the rules they made for their cultures, and so on.

The Book of Mormon is a record of God's dealings with a small group of His people, and it can best be appreciated through seeking a testimony of its truthfulness and its application to our lives now – NOT by studying the (already rather convincing) evidence surrounding it. As another testimony of Jesus Christ, its purpose is not to provide the world with yet another ancient record. As the different authors of the various books that it contains repeatedly remind us, its purpose is to bring us to Christ. If somehow, somewhere, an unmistakable fragment of the Nephite civilization somehow miraculously survived 1,600 years of earthquakes, volcanic eruptions, and jungle encroachment, well, that would be wonderful.

However, it's certainly not necessary, nor actually even important.

Evolving Paradigms

Don't hold your breath.

Six hundred years ago, everyone in Europe knew the world was flat. One could go outside and look at the sea or a wind-swept plain and say "of course – it *looks* flat, it must *BE* flat." Greek scientist-philosophers two millennia earlier (summarized by Eratosthenes and Aristotle) already knew otherwise. They had observed that the Earth's shadow on the Moon during a Lunar eclipse was round, and that visitors traveling to southern Egypt had observed that the Sun was at a different angle – it reached vertically down into the bottom of a well at noon – than at Athens on the same day of the year.

These and other observations clearly proved that the Earth was round, but the idea didn't take off, to use modern language. When Magellan's lone surviving caravel finally made it back to Lisbon after circumnavigating the Earth east-to-west, the ship's log was inexplicably one day behind Lisbon. Everyone was certain that they had made careful entries every day in the correct order. Hmmm.

One of us once flew in a Supersonic Concorde from London to Virginia, and from 20 miles up the sky is dead black at mid-day, and the horizon is quite noticeably curved. Everyone (almost everyone) believes the Earth is round now. That is called a paradigm-shift: everyone's idea or understanding of reality changes. Usually it means that the new explanation, or paradigm, better explains what we can observe.

People during the medieval period also thought the Earth was the center of everything; the Sun and Moon rotated around it, and Man was the most important thing on the Earth. It sure looked like Earth was the center. There was a real problem explaining the jinking paths of the planets as observers on the Earth saw them, however, until Kepler and others made the convincing argument that those paths could be explained rather nicely if you just gave up the Earth-centered paradigm for a Sun-centered paradigm. Kepler and Galileo both paid dearly for this, as they got seriously cross-wise with the Catholic Church over this claim.

Another slooooooowwwww paradigm-shift.

In the early 20th Century, Einstein proposed first his Special Theory of Relativity, and later his General Theory of Relativity. He did this by means of a Gedankenexperiment – German for a "thought experiment." It took a long time for physicists to accept that time could slow, that light could bend in empty space, and that no frame of reference was anchored.

This paradigm shift, like any other, was resisted – the idea that the speed of light was the only thing firm or fixed in the universe. Well, at least one could count on *something* being fixed. When things get tough to comprehend, physicists tend to "revert" to mathematical formalisms. We can explain relativity much easier with just a few equations – it's much easier with math than trying to explain how my evil twin ended up being younger when he flew to Alpha Centauri and back at 99% of the speed of light.

This new paradigm shift, though fiercely argued, happened quite a bit more rapidly than previous shifts. We had better means to communicate: scientific papers than were the norm in 1905 when Einstein first published. Again, humankind had a new, improved version of "reality," which we're now going to start putting in quotes.

As we wrote earlier, relativity is no longer a theory, but rock-hard tested and repeatedly proven. During a solar eclipse in 1919 light from a distant star was shown to bend – something that even made the front page of the New York Times (Dyson et al., 1920). Today, precise clocks on GPS satellites have to be very carefully corrected for the "frame drag" of relativity, because of their velocity relative to the hand-held GPS devices that we used to locate grasshopper traps and position geo-electrical soundings inside Mount St Helens' crater.

In the 1920's the idea of quantum mechanics arose to explain non-classical behavior observed in elementary particles and light. The expression "non-classical" essentially means that it was hard to wrap your head around the concepts that arose: particles had characteristics of waves and vice-versa, and Heisenberg showed that you couldn't pin down *both* location and momentum of an elementary particle at the same time. Also, an electron was not a charged point particle, but instead it acted like a wave-function, or *probability cloud* wrapped around a proton to make a hydrogen atom. It didn't sound clear and straightforward, like balls dropping from the Tower of Pisa, or apples from a tree.

After 1945, everyone started idolizing physicists – these guys could make that mumbo-jumbo actually *do* something (such as kill ~220,000 human beings with just two bombs). Most people could more easily wrap their heads around killing a lot of people and ending a protracted war. I guess we can believe the physicists from now on, was the new thinking.

But don't be in too much of a hurry here. Einstein really, *really* didn't like quantum mechanics. Sure, he could *understand* the math of Bohr, Heisenberg, Dirac, Fermi and others, but it just didn't... feel *right* to him.

Einstein resisted quantum mechanics until the day he died.

Some paradigm-shifting here, but more for some, less for others.

~~~~~

Let's ***Quick Jump to our newest 21st Century paradigms***. The paradigm-shifts have been coming fast and furiously the last 40 years:

- Black Holes exist.

- Continental Drift is happening – and causes volcanoes!

- Quantum Chromodynamics (QCD) describes hadrons (including protons and neutrons) and how they behave and interact.

- Cigarettes are _not_ good for your after-dinner digestion, but instead destroy your lungs, kill your heart, and prove that you were once stupid enough (like one of us) to start smoking.

- _Fuzzy_ Black Holes exist. Monster, Galaxy-Scale Black Holes exist. Black Holes can orbit other Black Holes. Black Holes can decrease and go away over trillions of years.

- Cancer is really caused by a few stem-cells inside a tumor, not most of the cells we call "cancer."

- Quantum entanglement has been observed, where particles know what a paired particle is doing faster than light can communicate between them.

- Complementarity – the idea that you can describe what's inside the Black Hole's Event Horizon (where you can't see anything because nothing, including light, can escape it) _or_ you can describe the Event Horizon itself – _but not both_. Because they are the same thing. Got that?

Wait! What's happening here? Physicists are moving away from proving things with tests and experiments and shifting back to promoting ideas like the 18th Century philosophers, most of which we can never know to be true because they can't be tested. If you don't need to test and measure things, you can publish papers much faster, get tenure more easily. Cynical? Perhaps.

So, what _is_ "reality"? At the most fundamental level, reality is something we understand via organic chemistry and weak electrical signals in nerves and axons between our retinas, our tympani, our fingers, our olfactory nerves, and our brains. Some theoretical physicists are swinging back to that old philosophical concept that we can never really know what reality truly is because of the primitive organic means we have of touching/hearing, tasting/smelling, and seeing it. That idea was first broached centuries ago by several philosophers, so... full circle?   Not quite.

There are several take-aways here:

First, treat anything that we physicists (or drug researchers) tell you to be the truth with a 200-mg dose of healthy suspicion – because what any physicist or cosmologist or biologist hangs her hat on today could be thrown out tomorrow for a new paradigm just as surely as you and I breathe. For starts, don't take the multiple universes ("multiverse") idea seriously. The same holds for the fundamentally un-falsifiable String Theory. *They can never be tested.*

Second, don't take seriously any ridicule from a scientist for being a believer in a faith tradition – for she/he is doing the very same thing. Come *on!* Who's doing the un-verifiable believing here?

Six Days

Why are we so fixated on time, anyway?

The first chapter of Genesis lays out in poetic manner a six-day sequence for the creation of the Earth. It's very simple, something that we imagine unschooled shepherd-astronomers could easily deal with, at least up to the time of Copernicus. However, 19th Century geologists in Europe (especially England – the British Geologists Association formed in 1858) had watched and measured as sediments accumulated in puddles and lakes. They realized that they could rather easily calculate the rate of sediment accumulation. They had also seen and mapped huge stacks of similar, consolidated sediments in many places – layers and layers of solidified mud and sand. Some had even begun to correlate distinctive bedding sequences in one place with similar bedding sequences hundreds of kilometers away.

Ah, they concluded: these must have been the same bottom of the same ocean at the same time long ago. This permitted British geologists, blessed with the full range of geologic ages on one small island (older to the north in Scotland, younger to the south in Sussex), to figure out which layer sat on top of another layer. The lower layer must be older, and they figured that units below these must be older still. By the turn of the 20th Century, even conservative geologists looking at their section-thickness numbers had concluded that the Earth had to be many millions of years old.

Not six days.

Geologists could also see another kind of time-line: progressively more sophisticated fossils, remains of ancient life forms not currently found walking or swimming the Earth, as the sediments got younger. They were systematically more evolved or sophisticated towards the "top" of the stratigraphic stack. This rule held in England and on the other side of the English Channel on the European continent. A curator at the BYU Geology Museum once walked one of us through a series of dinosaur vertebrae, showing how with time the vertebrae became lighter but at the same time structurally stronger. This meant, he explained, that the dinosaurs could run faster. Evolution was right there, laid out in age-order for me in bones, in dusty trays, in the center of the BYU campus.

Then Pierre and Marie Curie, Henri Becquerel, and others discovered radioactive decay around the beginning of the 20th Century. They could measure a decay rate for a given amount of a particular element, and they could chemically extract the daughter products forming as a result of that decay. It's an easy step to measure the ratio of a radioisotope to its stable daughter products. So... one should be able to figure how long that particular crystal (a zircon, for example, containing both uranium and lead and the isotopic decay-steps in between) has been sitting in a rock since it solidified and crystalized out of a magma melt.

Whoa. The early geochronologists started coming up with HUGE numbers. As more and more rock units were sampled and dated, the push-back for an oldest rock – homing in on an origin of the Earth – passed into the hundreds of millions of years, and then billions of years.

Radiometric dating currently suggests that the Earth is 4.54 +/- 0.01 billion years old. As we write this, the oldest zircon age for a rock is about 4.37 Ga (Valley, 2014; note that scientists prefer "Ga", or "Gyr", because a "billion" to an American is a thousand million, whereas to a European it is a million million). Thus the age of the Earth is currently estimated from meteorites as 4.54×10^9 years ± 1% (Hedman, 2007).

If you multiply this by 365 days per year, this is 1,657,100,000,000 days, at least, that our favorite planet in some sort of solidified state has been orbiting our Sun. This number is not really comprehensible... no one can really count that high.

However, as you consider the actual physical processes involved, as we understand them from geology and astronomy, the age of the Earth certainly can't be this precise. There was a proto-planetary disk (junk swirling in space around the starting-up Sun), then gravitational clustering, then segregation, then a crust formed, modified repeatedly by continued heavy early bombardment of more debris and planetoids falling into the growing gravity-well of the new proto-planet that would become Earth. Later in the game there was a collision with another incoming proto-planet perhaps the size of Mars that led to disintegration, reconsolidation, and the formation of the Moon. So, it's unrealistic to place such a precise three-decimal-point age as a "start," or age, of the Earth. It makes more sense instead to point at the oldest piece of un-melted material ever found. The current record-holder (above) comes from the Jack Hills of Western Australia; however, the world record holder goes back and forth between Australia and Greenland. If you compare the mass and luminosity of the Sun to other stars, and especially if you age-date meteorites, it is apparent that the Solar System can't be much older than that.

Certainly, there are complications with radiometric dating; what constitutes "partial melting" for instance, that allows the parent-daughter element ratio to slide? On the short-time scale we use ^{14}C dating (good only up to about 45,000 years). However, the Carbon-14 creation rate in the atmosphere varies over time depending on the cosmic ray flux. You can correct for this – you can calibrate for this variable cosmic ray creation rate by using tree-rings to lock in a date. Radiometric dating also must necessarily make some assumptions, among them that the decaying radioisotope and its daughter products remain together for the entire time that the age is calculated for (in other words, there could be no re-melting of zircons holding lead and uranium), and also that the decay rate today is the same now as it was when the original material solidified out of a melt. It's more complicated than that, even, but at this point we're only quibbling about small plus-and-minus stuff.

This is a long way around saying that rather few people take the Six Days of Genesis as literal truth these days. Genesis is, after all, a translation of a translation, and the original writer had rather little experience with orbital mechanics, conservation of angular momentum, and the weak nuclear force. He also had a limited vocabulary to work with. Keep in mind that the inerrancy of the KJV Bible is a concept *that only dates back to the late 19th Century* (Stubbs, 2016; Campbell, 2010).

In this context, we found some interesting things in the writings of a number of Church of Jesus Christ Apostles who were also scholars.

For example, John A. Widtsoe wrote about the "vast periods of time" required for each class of animal to rise, dominate the Earth, and then become extinct (*"Joseph Smith as Scientist,"* manual distributed by the General Board of the YMMIA, Church of Jesus Christ of Latter-day Saints, 1908). This was before radiometric dating came into play, so Widtsoe was ahead of most of the scientists of his time.

Here's something even more specific, unlike anything we've seen in any other church doctrine:

"What is a day? It is a specified time period; it is an age, an eon, a division of eternity; it is the time between two identifiable events. And each day, of whatever length, has the duration needed for its purposes". –Bruce R. McConkie, Apostle of the Church of Jesus Christ of Latter-Day Saints, during General Conference, 1982.

A friend once pointed out an interesting quote from the astronomer Carl Sagan:

"How is it that hardly any major religion has looked at science and concluded "This is better than we thought! The Universe is much bigger than our prophets said, grander, more subtle, more elegant. God must be even greater than we dreamed"? Instead they say, "No, No, No! My god is

a little god, and I want him to stay that way." A religion, old or new, that
stressed the magnificence of the Universe as revealed by modern science
might be able to draw forth reserves of reverence and awe hardly tapped
by the conventional faiths. Sooner or later, such a religion will emerge".
– Carl Sagan, "Pale Blue Dot: A Vision of the Human Future in Space"
(1994).

This strongly suggests that agnostics and atheists can also receive personal revelation. A bit late for Sagan, perhaps, but that particular religion he was talking about has emerged already.

But let's put this all into perspective. Can you count to a million? Neither can we, so the difference between a million years and a billion years seems somewhat irrelevant, unless you are a geochronologist. When one of us was the chief scientist for volcano hazards of the US Geological Survey, he once allocated $250,000 toward instrumentation for a rock-dating laboratory in our Menlo Park, CA, research center. He did this because it is critically important to know how long ago a volcanic eruption had taken place, in order to get a sense in real numbers for how dangerous that particular volcano might be today. You can then PLAN. This all assumes that the past is the key to the future, of course – another one of those taken-on-faith assumptions made by us scientists.

Getting a volcanic eruptive sequence dated is therefore pretty important, right? Especially if you live in, say, Seattle, or Tokyo, or anywhere under the shadow of a brooding volcano in the Mediterranean, or around the Pacific Rim.

But consider this: allow for a minute the possibility that there is life after life. We have agnostic friends, even atheist friends, who go back and forth on this one. We ourselves have a number of strong experiential reasons for no longer questioning this. If you are an atheist, then the Age of the Earth doesn't matter. If you are faith-based, then... well, it doesn't really matter to you, either. It's sort of like Pascal's Wager, discussed earlier.

When we die and make that transition across the Veil (or through the door or whatever you want to call it), we suspect there may be some questions asked of us. Like: *"Where is your family?"* Or, maybe, *"What did you do to help others?"*

Somehow, we don't think that anyone is going to ask us: *"While you were in your mortal state, what was your opinion about the age of the Earth?"*

2.555 Ga

Yet another remarkable "coincidence"

That number is an estimate given by W.W. Phelps for the age of the universe ("eternity") early in the 19th Century. Incidentally, "Ga" or "Gy" is the usual scientific shorthand for 1,000,000,000 years, because there is both a Short Scale and a Long Scale version of what a "billion" is. They differ, depending on the country you live in, by 1,000 (see previous chapter).

In "The Times & Seasons" newspaper, in 1835, Phelps wrote "...that eternity, agreeably to the records found in the catacombs of Egypt, has been going on in this system, (not this world) almost two thousand five hundred and fifty-five millions of years..."

A deeper probe suggests that Phelps came up with this number by multiplying

7,000 x 365 x 1,000 = 2,555,000,000 (Lewis, 2013).

In the statement, Phelps specifically said this was the age of the universe ("not this world"). This number also includes Phelps' assumptions that we are nearly at the end of eternity, that a day for the Lord was 1,000 years to man, and that Genesis supported a 7,000 year span of creation. The current best estimate for the age of the universe – the time since the Big Bang – is about 13.8 Gy. You can tie yourself up in knots over this half-order-of-magnitude difference, but on the scale of really important things, this ranks well below the noise threshold.

This 2.555 Gy number is nevertheless interesting, because the Great Oxygenation Event (GOE) of the Earth closely brackets this age. Depending on who writes about this, the GOE started at 2.7 Gy or 2.5 Gy, or 2.4 Gy (see Zahnle, et al., 2007). It is very difficult to pin a date this far back very closely at all, as most geologic evidence that far back is extremely fragmentary. Before the GOE, the Earth's atmosphere was largely methane, sulphur dioxide, carbon dioxide, and ammonia. The sky was not blue, and the Earth would have been unrecognizable to us as such. There are deposits of alluvial pyrite (FeS) sand found in Archean rocks in South Africa that predate the GOE; the grains are rounded, something that could never happen in the presence of oxygen (golden-yellow pyrite would turn rapidly to iron oxides, including rust, in the rough-and-tumble erosion and deposition process in the presence of oxygen).

A paper published in Space Science Reviews (the same Zahnle et al., 2007) fleshed out a lot of the chemistry necessary for oxygen to appear in the primordial Earth's atmosphere. First, a lot of hydrogen had to escape the atmosphere. This can happen when hydrogen-based molecules in the atmosphere decompose in the presence of ultraviolet light – and in the absence of a protective ozone (O_3) layer this happens easily. Then, a lot of the freed-up oxygen would be needed to break down the remaining methane in the atmosphere. There is another big oxygen sink, however: the rocks of the Earth's crust themselves had to be oxygenized. Only then (after the oxygen sinks in the crust, like iron, were filled) would significant amounts of O_2 get into the atmosphere. Only then would a significant amount reach the upper Troposphere and thus form that radiation-protective shell of ozone that allows life to flourish on the Earth.

Somewhere in this evolving planetary atmosphere, photosynthesis also began producing oxygen, but Zahnle et al. discounted photosynthesis as a significant producer until after the Huronian glaciation (the so-called "Snowball Earth") event, estimated to be between 2.4 to 2.1 Gy.

Today, modern photosynthesis in plants could produce the 21% oxygen in the modern atmosphere in just 2,000 years. During the Cretaceous, the ultimate dinosaur wonderland (or nightmare alley, depending on your point of view, or your size), the atmospheric oxygen ranged up to 35% – which would go a long way towards explaining 20-meter-long dinosaurs and meter-long insects in the fossil record from that time (Gale, 2001). The Earth's age may be around 4.5 Ga, but "as we presently understand it," it is closer to 2.555 Gy.

That could be just another remarkable coincidence, but we think it's yet another example of science-religion convergence.

A Farewell to Arms

Everything is getting better. We can prove this with statistics.

The essence of science is to gather data, and then to evaluate and weigh it, and finally to draw certain conclusions that the data can support. A book published not long ago (Pinker, 2011) makes an interesting claim:

Violence has declined throughout history, and still is declining today.

Wait a minute. What about the First World War? The Second World War? The deaths of 20,000,000 people during Stalin's purges in the 1930's? The 70,000,000 who starved to death under Mao in the 1960's Great Leap Forward? Two million people in American jails? What about 9/11? The Iraq, Afghanistan, Libyan, and Syrian Forever-Wars?

As Franklin Pierce Adams supposedly pointed out, "Nothing is more responsible for the good old days than a bad memory." (https://quoteinvestigator.com/2018/05/04/old-days/) In fact, this is how time proximity weight-loads the history that we remember, and it's why a good scientist scrupulously keeps records. This mistaken perception of growing violence is dramatically amplified by the rise of the 24-hour news cycle since the advent of CNN. This is called a *"bias towards recency."* A careful statistical and historical analysis makes a compelling case that, in fact, human-on-human violence has declined throughout history.

Put another way: the actual likelihood of being assaulted or killed has been falling for centuries.

How could this possibly be?

Pinker's book moves through the historical record first. Ever hear of the Thirty Years War? This represents continual European warfare, famine, and up to 11,000,000 deaths from 1618 to 1648. What about the Qing conquest of the Ming dynasty (1618 to 1683), with an estimated 25,000,000 deaths? The Mongol conquests – up to 40,000,000 deaths... and we are not even counting the estimated 200,000,000 deaths from the Black Plague that was arguably started by this.

Pinker then addresses the intellectual revolutions of the last several centuries, and even delves into modern studies on the human mind and human behavior. Pinker's lasting achievement is that his intellectual quest really knew no bounds: he covers the gamut from psychology, neuroscience, evolutionary biology, history, and social science.

Pinker didn't operate in a vacuum, however. He gives full credit to a particular inspiration. He calls Norbert Elias (1897 – 1990), a German-born scholar who wrote during Hitler's 1930's, "the most important thinker you have never heard of."

Elias proposed that the growth of the nation-state all over the world in the past several millennia has had profound effects (first described in Thomas Hobbes' 1651 book *"Leviathan"*) on stabilizing human behavior. It created physical boundaries, it established behavioral norms and attached consequences to bad behavior (Elias, 1939). The consequences were profound, too: increasingly over time outlaw behavior drew out the posse – it stirred up the hornet's nest – and sociopaths were consistently removed from the gene pool.

In the United States, we incarcerate more than 2,000,000 people, mostly men, but in past centuries there weren't resources to hold people in jail. Beheading, hanging, and feathering with arrows and burying in a bog (remember the fate of Tolund Man? ...of Ötzi the Ice Man?) accomplished the same goal, but much less expensively: society was made safe. With time, violent tendencies have been steadily filtered out of the human race, and all of this stemmed from the establishment of nation-states.

Another way of viewing this is that the Adversary is *not* winning his war with humanity. He's certainly losing the physical part of the war.

The other thing that Elias and Pinker noted as being crucial was the rise of commerce. Mutual gains from trade created a common purpose and raised most of humanity above the tribal state. Rising water floats all the boats at the same time. The xenophobia common throughout the world earlier – tribal defensiveness – became progressively less tenable. Xenophobia and killings associated with it interfered with the common gain and have been increasingly less tolerated by the majority of humanity.

There has also been a "rights revolution" in the past century: women's rights, civil rights, gay rights, animal rights, with the accompanying increase in sensitivity and empathy that goes with these. Another way to word this: there has been steady growth of Christ-like behavior in the past several centuries. That's not really surprising if you are a member of the Church of Jesus Christ.

Elias and Pinker also offer a somewhat more controversial idea: that there has been a rise in human reasoning ability. Certainly, IQ and equivalent scores have been steadily rising in the past 70 or so years (Flynn, 1987). However, this is hard to separate from evolving culture and even nutrition. Pinker also tends to dismiss income inequality as not causing serious damage to this growing world peace. However, numerous studies have shown that income inequality correlates closely with homicide rates in country after country, and even in areas within countries (think of

Chicago), independent of religion or culture (Krahn and others, 1986; Fajnzylber et al., 2002). If you wish to see low rates of violence (the anomalous Breivik massacre in 2012 notwithstanding) go to Norway. Norway has an income range far smaller than the United States or even many other countries in Europe, and it is one of the most peaceful nations on the planet. Everyone is pretty much the same – so there is less alienation and xenophobia.

So why do we perceive that things are getting worse? Part of the answer comes from the very nature of journalism, captured in the words of Journalist Eric Pooley, *"If it bleeds, it leads"* (http://evaluatingconversations.weebly.com/if-it-bleeds-it-leads.html). You may have read the satirical headline from *The Onion*: "CNN Holds Morning Meeting to Decide What Viewers Should Panic About For Rest of Day."

As Pinker put it in a recent TED talk,

> *"...bad things can happen quickly, but good things aren't built in a day. The papers could have run the headline, '137,000 people escaped from extreme poverty yesterday' every day for the last 25 years. That's one and a quarter billion people leaving poverty behind, but you never read about it"*
> (https://www.ted.com/talks/steven_pinker_is_the_world_getting_better_or_worse_a_look_at_the_numbers/transcript?language=en#t-49117).

Something neither Elias nor Pinker noted was an additional factor that we have noticed: the establishment of sports as a normative social activity. Sports in aggregate constitute a legally-sanctioned opportunity to compete with others without loss of life or limb (with rugby, hockey, and lacrosse as possible exceptions). Sports are a way to release pent-up energy and frustration; they are also a means for organizing small armies and using intellectual strategies to win... and gain fame and riches at the same time. The fact that almost no one dies is a nice side effect.

The bottom line is that the inherent angels in our natures seem to be winning the battle for the soul of humanity. Pinker is not a Theist; he would consider himself a Humanist, however. As such, he does not consider – even look at – religious aspects of this world-wide trend.

Largely thus overlooked is the part that Jesus Christ and His Restored Church have had in this evolution.

Why Did He Do That? *HOW Did He Do That?*

It all comes down to this.

One of us grew up as a Catholic, and recalls the nuns trying to explain the Nicaean Trinity idea to 11-year-old kids as "a great mystery." They expected us kids to accept the Trinity as something intrinsically incomprehensible (it clearly was to them) – but to nevertheless appreciate "the beauty of it" (as they apparently did). I remember being bothered by this at the time, but I was awash in a lot of other things that bothered me, all of which eventually led me to agnosticism and then to full-blown militant atheism. I don't recall ever hearing anything said about Christ's Atonement in eight years of Catholic elementary and junior high school. There was a lot of emphasis on the crucifixion, on death in general, and there were a lot of gruesome statues and images to get that death part across. You may miss this in some modern churches, but a tour through St Peter's Basilica in Rome will leave you with a sharp awareness of death and physical corruption. Death is everywhere, from the skeletal statuary to a rotting corpse behind glass, beneath an altar in the middle of the north nave.

For 10 years I was an atheist, and the subject of the Atonement never rose to my attention, any more than it had when I was a Catholic schoolboy. My earliest awareness of the Atonement as a newly minted Member of the Church of Jesus Christ was mostly one of curiosity: Why did Christ have to do that? And what *exactly happened*, anyway? Initially I accepted the idea that something important had been done – done for me as an individual – and that I should be grateful for it, but I really didn't understand it. I gradually came to accept that the sacrament ordinance was mainly there to keep the memory of Christ's sacrifice in the forefront of our minds, and to remember our own baptismal covenants, on a weekly basis.

I listened to General Authorities talk about the Atonement, and discovered LDS Institute classes, where I could ask questions of some people who knew a great deal more than I did. I was both relieved and at the same time mildly bothered that they had *also* thought long and hard about the Atonement a lot, but that they also didn't fully understand it either. This strongly implied that it was intrinsically not comprehensible, at least to someone like me. I've talked with Church members who are very relaxed about their faith. Doctrinal details that they do not understand are not a problem – they already have strong testimonies of the truth of it from other sources. I envy them because, unfortunately, that sort of calm faith didn't come to me easily. I still had a feeling that I must be missing something, because the atonement didn't yet *seem* to fit into the well-ordered, internally consistent understanding that I had found in the rest of Church doctrine. However, as a Conservation Law it did make fundamental sense: something had to be paid for. There is no such thing as a free lunch. Nothing comes free – SOMEONE must pay for everything in this life. That's basically the "conservation" in Conservations Laws like mass-energy, momentum, angular momentum, etc.

I was still stuck, but I fell back on the old idea that if you don't understand something, you can either invoke magic – or accept the fact that you are missing some critical information.

For me – for both of us – it could only be the latter, because as scientists we are not built for accepting "mysteries," though we *can* accept unanswered questions. For us a "mystery" is just something that can't be explained with the available evidence. It suggests an intractable problem – like being unable to predict earthquakes. For any scientist, a "mystery" is sort of like driving a car with something missing, perhaps a fender, or a window, or maybe even a tire. Mysteries and gaps in understanding make any scientist uneasy: the ordered world, the complete understanding (or at least an apparent symmetry) is missing – and it bothers us.

> 21 And now behold, my brethren, what natural man is there that knoweth these things? I say unto you, there is none that knoweth these things, save it be the penitent.
> 22 Yea, he that repenteth and exerciseth faith, and bringeth forth good works, and prayeth continually without ceasing-unto such it is given to know the mysteries of God; yea, unto such it shall be given to reveal things which never have been revealed... – Alma 26: 21-22

That sure sounds like part of an instruction manual. Repent (avoid or at least minimize sin in the first place is even better), exercise faith (i.e., don't blow something off because you don't immediately understand it), and pray consistently – these all seem to be keys to opening the door.

With multiple readings of the New Testament, I began to notice a number of subtleties. As a scientist, this was observing and gathering evidence on my part. There were clues in how soberly Christ approached the death process, for instance. He clearly understood well ahead of time that He was facing something much more than just death. There are some even more distinct clues in the manner in which He dealt with the hideous brutality of being slowly killed in the characteristically-engineered Roman manner. I noted that Christ was calm, subdued, and remarkably accepting as He was dragged from Caiaphas to Pilate to Herod and back to Pilate again. Quietly He dragged his cross until physical exhaustion overcame Him. There is no record of how He reacted to the nails being driven into his hands and feet, nor to how he struggled to breathe while on the cross. His words on the cross are recorded, but they are few, and these suggest that He was meek and quiet even during the brutal crucifixion.

The breathing – suffocation – aspect during a crucifixion is not trivial, by the way. The Romans (excellent engineers) had worked hard and experimented for centuries to develop the most drawn-out and gruesome way to terminate a human life. However, they had also learned how to shorten the process when necessary – by breaking the legs of the victim, which caused a quick death. The victim on the cross could then no longer stretch up to gather another breath, so he suffocated, or else died of shock. But the record says that Christ died at the ninth hour, well before sunset when the soldiers came to break the legs of the two thieves. A quick spear-thrust in His side brought forth a mixed fluid that indicates the blood was already separated by gravity into different components.

I believe that Christ was calm and accepting through the "trial" and crucifixion *because the hard part was already behind Him.* The hard part had actually occurred the night before, out of sight of His closest friends and disciples. Christ faced this mostly by himself, though Luke (only) indicates that he was strengthened at one point by an angel. What happened in that garden was so hard, in fact, that there were unusual manifestations of the stress that He was undergoing: blood dripping from his pores, the first plaintive emotion shown, expressed towards his disciples because they couldn't stay awake with Him through it, the emotional pleading to his Father in Heaven. Please, oh please let this pass by me.

Whatever happened – this great and unfathomable miracle – took place in the space of just a few hours, and it was very localized: A planetary balancing act happened in a small corner of a hilltop east of Jerusalem.

I'm still a long way from understanding the Atonement fully. I suspect that I may not even understand it completely until I get back to the Other Side. At least in part this is because I don't have a mind that can be aware of a near-infinite number of people at the same time. But I do understand, though imperfectly, that it was so hideously terrible that subsequent brutal treatment and a crucifixion the following day apparently paled by comparison.

As a scientist I can only draw inferences from the scriptures/data available to me, which are incomplete. Repeatedly, we read that Christ died for our sins. What does that really mean? I can understand the mass balancing principle: acts have consequences, and bad acts have bad consequences, and they are cumulative. The conservation laws that are fundamental to the ordered operation of the universe are all consistent: there is nothing that is "free," everything must be paid for. All processes must balance out. In chemistry, carbon dioxide + water + energy = glucose + oxygen. In physics, $E = mc^2$.

Unfortunately, there are no human adults who can realistically pay back all the bad things they have done. No one of us could ever pay the full price for the damage our careless (or deliberate) cruelties or inconsideration have caused in any given week, much less in a lifetime. No one of us can restore to life a person we killed, restore a marriage we destroyed, or heal a child we permanently scarred.

The Second Law of Thermodynamics, sometimes called entropy, might help explain why: It's impossible to restore a broken egg. Entropy: mix black and white sand and see entropy at work. Then try to reverse it. Entropy cannot be reversed unless a prodigious amount of energy is brought to bear, and then only locally, as in the example of photosynthesis above, where light energy is required to balance the chemical equation and bring order to the chemical stew.

Maybe this is a clue to understanding the atonement: somehow, Christ accomplished that mass balance. Let's try to be analytic here: as many as 108,000,000,000 human beings currently live or have once lived on this planet (Haub, 2011). How can a single individual fix the damage incurred during the lives of at least 100,000,000,000 people? If we apply the natural laws of balance to our understanding of the Atonement, Christ's suffering has to balance out all the rest, like the "Light Energy" in that equation.

He died for our sins. That means He had to deal with our sins. It seems to me that means that He must have witnessed and somehow *confronted* all of our sins. Since I was an early teen, I have studied the Second World War and have been horrified by the cruelties of the Holocaust – and, for that matter, any and every war. Killing a single individual can be harrowing to even try to comprehend. It is remarkably difficult to destroy a human being – we humans are so resilient, so built to survive almost everything, that it takes quite a lot of brutal effort to kill us. What about a whole life's worth of injury or carelessness by a single individual? What about 100,000,000,000 times that?

There is another terrifying inference to this line of thinking: Christ must have witnessed everything that *I* did to this point in my life – and everything I will ever do. This seems to defy causality, but we already know that the arrow of time is not as simple as most scientists had long thought it to be.

> *"And it may suffice if I only say they are preserved for a wise purpose, which purpose is known unto God; for he doth counsel in wisdom over all his works, and his paths are straight, <u>and his course is one eternal round</u>* (emphasis mine)." – Alma 37:12

This conclusion follows from the necessity to balance and pay for everything explicit in the Atonement. I didn't arrive at this understanding until I was already in my 30's. When I finally got there, the thought appalled me. So much so, in fact, that it took me quite a bit less time to resolve that I will do *everything in my power to not add to what He had to face in Gethsemane.*

There is more to the atonement than balancing or paying for sin, however. Somehow Christ also confronted – and compensated for – *all of our individual personal suffering*, giving us the right to reach out for and receive peace (if not a full immediate understanding) when we suffer pain or sorrow, including the loss of a loved one. Most readers have experienced that "*peace that surpasseth understanding*" (Phillip 4:7).

These are some of the things I think about during a Sacrament meeting.

Now we come to the final issue: why was He willing to do this? This is actually less difficult to understand than the balancing part, once we comprehend His love for us. The scriptures make it clear that Christ had perfectly aligned His mind and thinking with that of our Heavenly Father. "I and my Father are One" (John 10:30). This was not forced, it was a free-will alignment. Christ arrived on this Earth as an infant, but as He grew, He learned what He had to do "Line upon line, precept upon precept..." (2Nephi 28:30) – so it's something that we too can do. Just as we as parents would be willing to die to save even one of our children.

That's why! *Exactly* like our Father in Heaven, Jesus Christ has and always will care about us. He cares deeply about each of us, as a father or mother would. It is no coincidence then that families are the fundamental core of our civil society, of our eternal society. One important element of the family is that it helps us, however vaguely, to comprehend that love.

Infinite love is certainly more on a scale with 100,000,000,000 times the love we feel for our own children.

The mass balance does require something of us, however: a meek and contrite spirit, ever greater humility, a steady increase in Christ-like behavior and thinking – or at least progress in that direction. It anticipates determined avoidance of further sin.

In other words, we are required only to do just exactly what each of us can manage to do.

OUR part is clear then: we understand enough now to take toddler steps to follow Christ's pure example, and never, never, add more to what He faced on that dark hill east of Jerusalem.

Epilogue

Why did we write this book?

We have both been struck, when someone dies, by how many people say to the grieving survivors, "Our thoughts are with you." Some may say "Our prayers are with you," but it's really the same thing. Everyone feels helpless and wants to think that they can somehow say something that will have some efficacy. *Everyone* hopes that there might be some sort of immortality, though some settle for the rather weak version that their writings or published books – or even good deeds – will somehow serve that purpose. That they will be remembered at all, for more than a few years, is a remarkable conceit if you just consider the historical record.

We have both also been struck at how many people – atheists, agnostics, and believers – will start their thinking framework with some profound, and unsupportable, assumptions:

- God exists.
- There is no God.
- A*B = B*A.
- We just somehow came into our complex existence from nothing, contrary to the Second Law of Thermodynamics.
- There are 26 precisely-tuned-for-life fundamental physical constants that we do not understand but accept anyway.
- There are quadrillions of parallel universes out there (the multiverse) that we can never detect, never test for, and with an unknown source for all that matter and energy.
- There are physical laws governing the universe... and we just accept them.

It seems that everyone somehow knows a lot of things a priori. They just "feel" something to be true, they have an "intuition" ... and both atheists and believers can be _very_ certain about these assumptions. The most prominent book-writing atheists derive an awful lot of their personal beliefs from somewhere, and their arguments to defend them are frankly indistinguishable in substance from those of someone from a faith tradition. Both atheists and believers are sometimes guilty of using scorn as a tactical bullying weapon to shame converts to their viewpoint.

They – we – are all intuitively recognizing something that we can put a name to: personal revelation. Judeo-Christian tradition implicitly recognizes that some of us can do this – actually receive correct information directly from a Supreme Being. But why would the prophets continue for millennia, and then suddenly cease after 70 AD? That just makes no sense to us.

We are scientists by profession. As such we have known surprisingly few fellow scientists who believe science is the End of All Things and make it their personal religion – yet there are the occasional book-writing biologists and physicists out there who do. They are not gentle towards people from a faith tradition, nor even especially toward philosophers.

On the other extreme, there are people like Austrian philosopher Paul Feyerabend (1924-1994) who

> *"...even gave up altogether on a so-called scientific method, arguing that science is not a special technique for producing truth but a flawed species of regular human reasoning (loaded with error, bias and rhetorical persuasion)."* (Catapano and Critchley, 2016, p. 368)

We fall somewhere between these two extremes of the spectrum. We are both scientists, and believe strongly that science is one of the best paths to finding truth, even if you separate it from technology and engineering. However, we are aware that science is very, very human, and with that human-ness it has lots of flaws.

We nevertheless hope we have shown in this book that truth is things that are correct, that can be and have been tested and verified. Also, we hope we have shown that truth is crucial to success: you have the right to believe that 1 + 1 = 3, but your mathematics based on that premise will not land a man on the Moon. We hope we have shown that there are at least three paths to get to the Ultimate Truth, to answer the Big Questions, and these are science, religion, and philosophy. History may be called a fourth path, perhaps, because like philosophy it enforces honesty. Each path appears to be imperfect, incomplete, or at least can achieve only so much and only in certain domains. Stephen J. Gould called these "Non-Overlapping Magisteria" (Gould, 1997). However, we believe the evidence presented in this book shows that The Big Three are converging (in some cases rapidly) on a larger Ultimate Truth, a Truth with a capital "T", and by that we mean an understanding that encompasses *all things that are correct*.

As best we can tell, you can get there faster if you work all three paths at the same time.

REFERENCES

Abrams, Elliot M., 1994, How the Maya Built Their World: University of Texas Press, 192 pp. ISBN 978-0-292-70462-6.

Ackermann, Eric, 2006, Indicators of failed information epidemics in the scientific journal literature: A publication analysis of Polywater and Cold Nuclear Fusion: Scientometrics, 66 (3), p. 451–466. doi:10.1007/s11192-006-0033-0

Ale-Agha, Niloofar; Christine Goy; Philipp Jakobs; Ioakim Spyridopoulos; Stefanie Gonnissen; Nadine Dyballa-Rukes; Karin Aufenvenne; Florian von Ameln; Mark Zurek; Tim Spannbrucker; Olaf Eckermann; Sascha Jakob; Simone Gorressen; Marcel Abrams; Maria Grandoch; Jens W. Fischer; Karl Köhrer; René Deenen; Klaus Unfried; Joachim Altschmied; and Judith Haendeler, 2018, CDKN1B/p27 is localized in mitochondria and improves respiration-dependent processes in the cardiovascular system— New mode of action for caffeine: PLOS Biology (open access), Published: June 21, 2018 https://doi.org/10.1371/journal.pbio.2004408

Ambrose, Stanley H., 1998, Late Pleistocene human population bottlenecks, volcanic winter, and differentiation of modern humans: Journal of Human Evolution 34 (6): p. 623–651.

Ambrose, Stephen E, 1997, Undaunted Courage: Simon & Schuster, 592 pp. ISBN 978-0-7434-7788-8

American Heart Association, 2014, Caffeine and Heart Disease: https://www.heart.org/en/healthy-living/healthy-eating/eat-smart/nutrition-basics/caffeine-and-heart-disease

Anonymous, 1956, Journal of Shipbuilding, Marine Engineering, Dock, Harbours & Shipping, 87, 1956, p. 422.

Anonymous, 2013, Trouble at the lab: The Economist magazine, October 19, 2013 issue. http://www.economist.com/news/briefing/21588057-scientists-think-science-self-correcting-alarming-degree-it-not-trouble/

Atwater, B.F., Musumi-Rokkaku, S., Satake, K., Tsuji, Y., Ueda, K., and Yamaguchi, D.K., 2015, The orphan tsunami of 1700—Japanese clues to a parent earthquake in North America, 2nd ed.: Seattle, University of Washington Press, and also U.S. Geological Survey Professional Paper 1707, 135 pp. doi:10.1017/S0016756807004098.

Ayers, Lewis, 2006, Nicaea and Its Legacy: Oxford University Press, 465 pp.
    ISBN 978-0-19-875505-0

Baer, James L., 1986, The Third Nephi Disaster: A Geological View:
    Dialogue: A Journal of Mormon Thought 19/1 (Spring 1986).

Ball, Russell H., 1993, An Hypothesis concerning the Three Days of
    Darkness Among the Nephites: Journal of Book of Mormon Studies
    2/1.

Barnes, Timothy D., 1981, Constantine and Eusebius: Harvard University
    Press, 458 pp. ISBN 978-0-674-16530-4.

Barrow, John D. and Frank J. Tipler, 1988, The Anthropic Cosmological
    Principle: Oxford University Press, 738 pp. ISBN 978-0-19-
    282147-8.

Bassett, Arthur, 1977, Now abideth these three: Ensign, September 1977
    issue https://www.lds.org/ensign/1977/09/now-abideth-these-
    three?lang=eng.

Begley, C. Glenn, and Lee M. Ellis, 2012, Reproducibility of research findings
    – Preclinical research generates many secondary publications,
    even when results cannot be reproduced: Nature 483, p. 531–533
    (29 March 2012 issue) doi:10.1038/483531a

Bishop, John G., Niamh B. O'Hara, Jonathan H. Titus, Jennifer L. Apple,
    Richard A. Gill, and Louise Wynn, 2010, N-P Co-Limitation of
    Primary Production and Response of Arthropods to N and P in
    Early Primary Succession on Mount St. Helens Volcano: PlosOne,
    doi:10.1371/journal.pone.0013598

Brown, Peter, 2003, The Rise of western Christendom, 2nd edition:
    Blackwell Publishing. 636 pp. ISBN 978-0-63-122138-8

Burchell, M.J., 2006, W(h)ither the Drake Equation?: International Journal
    of Astrobiology 5 (3), p. 243–250. doi:10.1017/S1473550406003107

Burnham, Robert, and David H. Levy, 2000, Great Comets: Cambridge
    University Press, p. 53, ISBN 0-521-64600-6.

Caldwell, R.R., R. Dave, and P.J. Steinhardt, 1998, Cosmological Imprint of
    an Energy Component with General Equation-of-State: Physical
    Review Letters 80 (8), p. 1582–1585.
    doi:10.1103/PhysRevLett.80.1582.

Campbell, Gordon, 2010, Bible – the story of the King James Version: Oxford
    University Press, Oxford, 368 pp. ISBN 978-0-19-955759-2.

Carson, Rachel, 1962, Silent Spring: Houghton-Mifflin, 378 pp. ISBN 0-
    618-25305-X

Caspari, Rachel, 2011, The evolution of grandparents: Scientific American, August 2011 issue https://www.scientificamerican.com/article/the-evolution-of-grandparents-2012-12-07/

Catapano, Peter, and Simon Critchley, 2016, The Stone Reader – Modern philosophy in 133 arguments: Liveright Publishing, New York, 794 pp.

Church of Jesus Christ of Latter-Day Saints Handbook 2, Administering the Church, Section 21 Administrative Policies 21.1.8

Cocconi, G.; Morisson, P.,1959, Searching for Interstellar Communications (PDF): Nature 184 (4690), p. 844–846. doi:10.1038/184844a0

Coe, Michael D.,1999, The Maya (6th ed.): Thames and Hudson, 256 pp. ISBN 0-500-28066-5

Connor, James A., 2006, Pascal's wager – the man who played dice with God: Harper, San Francisco, 180 pp. ISBN 9780060766917.

Cook, John, Dana Nuccitelli, Sarah A. Green, Mark Richardson, Bärbel Winkler, Rob Painting, Robert Way, Peter Jacobs, and Andrew Skuce, 2013, Quantifying the consensus on anthropogenic global warming in the scientific literature: Environmental Research Letters, 8, no.2, (15May 2013) http://iopscience.iop.org/article/10.1088/1748-9326/8/2/024024

Coyle, Harold P., 2014, Syzygy: in: Access Science, McGraw-Hill Education. doi:10.1036/1097-8542.757218

Crutzen, Paul J. and Stoermer, E.F., 2000, The "Anthropocene": Global Change Newsletter, 41, 17.

Crutzen, Paul J., 2002, Geology of mankind: Nature 415, 23 (3 January 2002) doi:10.1038/415023a

Darwin Correspondence Project: https://www.darwinproject.ac.uk/

Davenport, Coral, 2015, Nations Approve Landmark Climate Accord in Paris: New York Times. http://www.nytimes.com/2015/12/13/world/europe/climate-change-accord-paris.html

De Bruhl, Marshall, 2006, Firestorm: Allied Airpower and the Destruction of Dresden: Random House, 368 pp. ISBN 978-0679435341

De Groote, Michael, 2010, Mormon scholar explains the historical difficulty created by the Golden Plates: Deseret News, Oct. 29 2010 http://www.deseretnews.com/article/705362294/Mormon-scholar-explains-the-historical-difficulty-created-by-the-Golden-Plates.html?pg=all

DeWeerdt, Sarah, 2011, Prevention – activity is the best medicine: Nature 475, S16–S17 (14 July 2011) doi:10.1038/475S16a

Diamond, Jared, 2005, Collapse: How societies choose to fail or survive: Penguin Books, 592 pp. ISBN 978-0-241-95868-1

Diamond, Jared, 2002, Evolution, consequences and future of plant and animal domestication: Nature 418, p. 700-707 (8 August 2002). doi:10.1038/nature01019

Doxey, Roy W., 1986, What was the approximate weight of the gold plates from which the Book of Mormon was translated? Ensign, December 1986 issue. https://www.lds.org/ensign/1986/12/i-have-a-question?lang=eng#footnote3-03207_000_030.

Drake, Frank, 1961, https://en.wikipedia.org/wiki/Drake_equation

Droke, Maxwell, 1956, The Speaker's Handbook of Humor, Anecdote Number 1172, Title: Not Superstitious, Quote Page 373, Harper & Brothers Publishers, New York.

Dyson, F. W.; Eddington, A. S.; Davidson, C., 1920, A Determination of the Deflection of Light by the Sun's Gravitational Field, from Observations Made at the Total Eclipse of May 29, 1919: Philosophical Transactions of the Royal Society A: Mathematical, Physical and Engineering Sciences 220 (571-581), p. 291–333. doi:10.1098/rsta.1920.0009.

Eggertson, Laura, 2010, Lancet retracts 12-year-old article linking autism to MMR vaccines: Canadian Medical Association Journal, March 9, 2010 issue, 182 no. 4 doi: 10.1503/cmaj.109-3179

Einstein, A., 1905, On the Electrodynamics of Moving Bodies: Annalen der Physik 17, p. 891-921.
http://einsteinpapers.press.princeton.edu/vol2-trans/154

Eisenhauer, F., R. Schödel, R. Genzel1, T. Ott, M. Tecza, R. Abuter, A. Eckart, and T. Alexander, 2003, A Geometric Determination of the Distance to the Galactic Center: The Astrophysical Journal Letters, Volume 597, Number 2Astrophysical Journal Letters 597, Number 2, p. L121-L124.
http://iopscience.iop.org/article/10.1086/380188/meta;jsessionid=6548E6F06ACB9CF433E45FDE895E4895.c3.iopscience.cld.iop.org

Elias, Norbert, 1939, Über den Prozeß der Zivilisation. Soziogenetische und psychogenetische Untersuchungen. Erster Band. Wandlungen des Verhaltens in den weltlichen Oberschichten des Abendlandes and Zweiter Band. Wandlungen der Gesellschaft. Entwurf einer Theorie der Zivilisation. Basel: Verlag Haus zum Falken. (Published in English as Norbert, E., 1069, The Civilizing Process, v. I: The History of Manners, Oxford: Blackwell. And Norbert, E., 1969, The

Civilizing Process, v. II: State Formation and Civilization, Oxford: Blackwell.

Elliott, Austin, 2014, Tohoku tsunami maps: lessons for the Pacific Northwest: American Geophysical Union blogs http://blogs.agu.org/tremblingearth/2014/03/12/tohoku-tsunami-maps-lessons-for-the-pacific-northwest/

Ellis, George F.R., 2011, Does the Multiverse Really Exist: Scientific American, August 2011 issue, p. 35-43. http://www.relativitycalculator.com/articles/multiverse_exist_george_ellis/page_38.html

Eyring, Henry, Sr., 1967, Faith of a Scientist: Bookcraft, Salt Lake City, 175 pp.

Eyring, Henry, Sr., 1972, Science and religion: Henry Eyring Lecture Series, LDS Institute of Religion, University of Arizona. (no doi: link)

Eyring, Henry, Sr., 1983, Reflections of a Scientist: Deseret Book, 101 pp. ISBN 978-1-609-08285-7

Fajnzylber, Pablo; Daniel Lederman, and Norman Loayza, 2002, Inequality and Violent Crime: The Journal of Law & Economics, 45, 1 (April 2002), p. 1-39.

Fanelli, Daniele 2009, How many scientists fabricate and falsify research – A systematic review and meta-analysis of survey data: PLoS ONE 4(5): e5738. doi:10.1371/journal.pone.0005738

Flynn J. R., 1987, Massive IQ gains in 14 nations – What IQ tests really measure: Psychological Bulletin 101 (2): p. 171–191. doi:10.1037/0033-2909.101.2.171.

Frankel, Charles, 1999, The End of the Dinosaurs: Chicxulub Crater and Mass Extinctions: Cambridge University Press. 236 pp. ISBN 0-521-47447-7

Freedman, David H., 2010, Lies, damned lies, and medical science: The Atlantic magazine, November 2010 issue. http://www.theatlantic.com/magazine/archive/2010/11/lies-damned-lies-and-medical-science/308269/

Frieman, Joshua, 2011, Dark Energy – Theory and Observations; Dark Energy: Physics Today 64 (6), p. 53. doi:10.1063/1.3603920.

Gale, Joseph; Shimon Rachmilevitch; Joseph Reuveni; and Micha Volokita, 2001, The high oxygen atmosphere toward the end Cretaceous; a possible contributing factor to the K/T boundary extinctions and to the emergence of C4 species: Journal of Experimental Botany 52 (357), p. 801-809. doi:10.1093/jexbot/52.357.801

Gauch, Hugh G., 2003, Scientific Method in Practice, Cambridge University Press, 435 pp. ISBN 978-0-521-01708-4.

Gee, John, 1997, Notes and Communications – Another Note on the Three Days of Darkness: Journal of Book of Mormon Studies 6/2 (no doi: link)

Gerlach, Terry, 2011, Volcanic versus anthropogenic carbon dioxide: EOS, Transactions of the American Geophysical Union, 92, Issue 24, p. 201-202 (14 June 2011 issue), doi:10.1029/2011EO240001

Ghez, A.M., S. Salim, S. D. Hornstein, A. Tanner, J. R. Lu, M. Morris, E. E. Becklin, and G. Duchêne, 2005, Stellar orbits around the galactic center black hole: The Astrophysical Journal 620, Number 2, http://iopscience.iop.org/article/10.1086/427175/meta

Gibbons, Ann, 1993, Pleistocene Population Explosions: Science 262 (5130): p. 27–28. doi:10.1126/science.262.5130.27.

Givens, Terryl L., 2002, By the Hand of Mormon – The American Scripture That Launched a New World Religion: Oxford University Press, 310 pp. ISBN 0-19-513818-X

Goebbels, Josef, (1941) Die Zeit ohne Beispiel. Munich: Zentralverlag der NSDAP. p. 364-369 http://thinkexist.com/quotation/-if_you_tell_a_lie_big_enough_and_keep_repeating/345877.html

also: http://izquotes.com/quote/383851

also:

http://www.holocaustresearchproject.org/holoprelude/goebbels.html

Goethe, Wolfgang, 1832, Faustus Parts One and Two, translation: David Luke, Oxford World Classics, (a play). ISBN 978-0-19-953620-7

Goffard, Christopher, 2011, Harold Camping is at the heart of a mediapocalypse: Los Angeles Times. http://articles.latimes.com/2011/may/21/local/la-me-rapture-20110521/2 [Retrieved October 13, 2011]

Goldman, Jason G., 2010, Monday Pets – The Russian Fox Study: Scientific American blogs, June 14, 2010. https://blogs.scientificamerican.com/thoughtful-animal/monday-pets-the-russian-fox-study/

Gott III, J. Richard; Mario Jurić; David Schlegel; Fiona Hoyle; Michael Vogeley; Max Tegmark; Neta Bahcall; and Jon Brinkmann, 2005, A map of the universe: Astrophysical Journal 624 (2): p. 463–484. doi:10.1086/428890.

Gould, Stephan J., 1997, Nonoverlapping Magisteria: Natural History 106 (March 1997 issue): p. 16–22 (no doi: link)

Grimal, Nicolas, 1992, A History of Ancient Egypt: Blackwell Books, 256 pp. ISBN 978-0-63-117472-1

Grover, Jerry D., 2014, Geology of the Book of Mormon, Vinyard, UT (self-published), 233 pp.

Hamblin, William, 2015, Maya king lists: Mormon Channel – Enigmatic Mirror (blog) http://www.patheos.com/blogs/enigmaticmirror/2015/06/30/hamblin-21-maya-king-lists/ (Accessed 10 October 2016).

Harding, Sandra, 1976, Can theories be refuted – essays on the Duhem-Quine thesis: Springer Science & Business Media, 315 pp. ISBN 978-90-277-0630-0.

Haub, Carl, 2011, How Many People Have Ever Lived on Earth? Population Reference Bureau. http://www.prb.org/Publications/Articles/2011/HowManyPeopleHaveEverLivedonEarth.aspx

Hawking, Stephen, 2001, The universe in a nutshell: Bantam Spectra, 224 pp. ISBN 0-553-80202-X

Hedman, Matthew, 2007, Meteorites and the Age of the Solar System: in: The Age of Everything: University of Chicago Press. p. 142–162. ISBN: 978-02-263-2294-0

Held, J.; Wynn, L.; Reed, J.; and R. Wang, 2007, Supply requirement prediction during long duration space missions using Bayesian estimation: International Journal of Logistic Research And Applications 10, No. 4, p. 351–366. doi:10.1080/13675560701281396?journalCode=cjol20

Hildebrand, Alan R.; Penfield, Glen T.; Kring, David A.; Pilkington, Mark; Zanoguera, Antonio Camargo; Jacobsen, Stein B.; Boynton, William V., 1991, Chicxulub Crater; a possible Cretaceous/Tertiary boundary impact crater on the Yucatan Peninsula, Mexico: Geology 19 (9): p. 867–871. doi:10.1130/0091-7613(1991)019<0867:CCAPCT>2.3.CO;2.

Hilton, Lynn M.; and Hope A. Hilton, 1976, In Search of Lehi's Trail: Deseret Books, Salt Lake City, 148 pp. ISBN 978-0-877-47620-7

Horgan, J., 1992, Profile: Karl R. Popper – The Intellectual Warrior: Scientific American 267 (5): 38–44. doi:10.1038/scientificamerican1192-38.

Hosie, Rachel, 2018, Four cups of coffee a day linked to improved heart health, study finds: The Independent, https://www.independent.co.uk/life-style/health-and-families/coffee-four-cups-day-heart-health-conditions-study-caffeine-effects-a8411231.html

Hough, Susan, 2009, Predicting the Unpredictable: The tumultuous science of earthquake prediction: Princeton University Press, 260 pp. ISBN 978-0-691-13816-9

Interpreter Foundation, 2013, http://www.mormoninterpreter.com/events/2013-symposium-science-mormonism-cosmos-earth-man/bios-abstracts/

Ioannidis, John P., 2005a, Why most published research findings are false: PLoS Med. 2005 Aug; 2(8): e124. doi:10.1371/journal.pmed.0020124

Ioannidis John P., 2005b, How to make more published research true: PLoS Med. 2014 Oct 21; 11(10): e1001747. doi:10.1371/journal.pmed.1001747.

Jaffe, R., 2005, Casimir effect and the quantum vacuum: Physical Review D 72 (2): 021301. doi:10.1103/PhysRevD.72.021301

Jarvik, Elaine, 2006, Beliefs on Darwin's evolution vary from religion to religion: Deseret News, Published: Jan. 19, 2006. http://www.deseretnews.com/article/635177399/Beliefs-on-Darwins-evolution-vary-from-religion-to-religion.html?pg=all

Johnson, Arch C.; and Eugene S. Schweig, 1996, The enigma of the New Madrid earthquakes of 1811-1812: Annual Review of Earth and Planetary Science, 1996 (24) p. 339-384. doi:10.1146/annurev.earth.24.1.339

Johnson, Steven, 2006, The Ghost Map – The story of London's most terrifying epidemic – and how it changed science, cities and the modern world: Riverhead Books. p. 195–196. ISBN 1-59448-925-4.

Jordan, Benjamin R., 2003, Investigating New World Volcanism at the Time of Christ's Death: Insights 23/6. (no doi: link)

Kallinger, T.; Iliev, I.; Lehmann, H.; Weiss, W. W., 2005, The puzzling Maia candidate star Alpha Draconis: Proceedings of the International Astronomical Union. doi:10.1017/S1743921305009865

Karimi, Faith, 2015, With 1 male left worldwide, northern white rhinos under guard 24 hours: http://www.cnn.com/2015/04/16/africa/kenya-northern-white-rhino/index.html

Kolbert, Elizabeth, 2014, The Sixth Extinction, An Unnatural History: Henry Holt & Company, 319 pp. ISBN 978-0-805-09299-8

Kowallis, Bart J., 1999, In the Thirty and Fourth Year – A Geologist's View of the Great Destruction in 3 Nephi: BYU Studies 37/3. (no doi: link)

Krahn, Harvey; Timothy F. Hartnagel; and John W. Gartrell, 1986, Income Inequality And Homicide Rates – Cross-National Data And Criminological Theories: Criminology 24, 2, First published: May 1986 https://doi.org/10.1111/j.1745-9125.1986.tb01496.x

Kuhn, T.S., 1962, The structure of scientific revolutions: University of Chicago Press, 208 pp. ISBN 978-0-226-45811-3

Kutterolf, S.; A. Freundt; W. Peréz; T. Mörz; U. Schacht; H. Wehrmann; and H.-U. Schmincke, 2008, Pacific offshore record of plinian arc volcanism in Central America: 1. Along-arc correlations: Geochemistry, Geophysics, Geosystems, 27 pp. doi: 10.1029/2007GC001631

Leach, Adam, 2014, A Kingdom of riches – Saudi Arabia looks to strike it rich with mining sector: http://www.mining-technology.com/features/featurea-kingdom-of-riches-saudi-arabia-looks-to-strike-it-rich-with-mining-sector-4382267/ "The history of mining in the Kingdom of Saudi Arabia stretches back thousands of years. The first record of it has been dated to 2100 BC, while carbon dating has shown that operations at Madh Ad Dahab mine were underway at around 1000 BC. Archaeologists have claimed that a copper mine was generating revenue for King Solomon in the 10th century BC."

Lewis, John S., 2013, The Scale of Creation in Space and Time: The Interpreter Foundation: Science and Mormonism Symposium, Provo, November 2013. http://www.mormoninterpreter.com/events/2013-symposium-science-mormonism-cosmos-earth-man/bios-abstracts/#lewis

Lind, Don, 1973, Science and religion: Henry Eyring Lecture Series, LDS Institute of Religion, University of Arizona. (no doi: link; authors' copy)

Lipman, P.W.; and D.R. Mullineaux, eds., 1981, The 1980 Eruptions of Mount St. Helens, Washington: U.S. Geological Survey Professional Paper 1250, 844 pp. https://pubs.er.usgs.gov/publication/pp1250

Lyon, Joseph L., Kent Gardner, and Richard E. Gress, 1994, Cancer incidence among Mormons and non-Mormons in Utah (United States) 1971–85: Cancer Causes & Control 5, Issue 2, p. 149–156 doi:10.1007/BF01830261

MacMullen, R., 1984, Christianizing The Roman Empire A.D.100-400: Yale University Press, 183 pp. ISBN 0-300-03642-6

Maxwell-Stuart, P., 1997, Chronicle of the Popes – The Reign-by-Reign Record of the Papacy over 2000 Years: Thames and Hudson, London, 240 pp. ISBN 0-500-01798-0.

McBrien, Richard, 1997, Lives of the Popes – The Pontiffs from St. Peter to John Paul II: Harper, San Francisco, 528 pp. ISBN 0-06-065304-3.

McCabe, Joseph, 1939, A History of the Popes: Watts & Co., London, 516 pp. https://archive.org/details/historyofthepope014405mbp

Mitchell, Amy, Katerina Eva Matsa, Jeffrey Gottfried, and Jocelyn Kiley, 2014, Political Polarization & Media Habits: The Pew Research Center, (https://guides.lib.umich.edu/c.php?g=637508&p=4462444

Morrison, James, 1980, No one gets out of here alive: Plexus Publishing, 396 pp. ISBN 978-0446602280

Nemeroff, Charles B.; Dwight L. Evans; Laszlo Gyulai; Gary S. Sachs; Charles L. Bowden; Ivan P. Gergel; Rosemary Oakes; and Cornelius D. Pitts, 2001, Double-blind, placebo-controlled comparison of Imipramine and Paroxetine in the treatment of bipolar depression: American Journal of Psychiatry 158, p. 906-912. doi:10.1176/appi.ajp.158.6.906

Newhall, Christopher G., and Self, Stephen, 1982, The Volcanic Explosivity Index (VEI): An Estimate of Explosive Magnitude for Historical Volcanism": Journal of Geophysical Research 87 (C2): p. 1231–1238. doi:10.1029/JC087iC02p01231

Nibley, Hugh, 1967, Since Cumorah: Deseret Books, Salt Lake City, Utah. 528 pp. ISBN 978-0-87-579139-5

Hugh W. Nibley, 1986, Before Adam, In: Hugh W. Nibley, Old Testament and Related Studies (Vol. 1 of Collected Works of Hugh Nibley), edited by John W. Welch, Gary P. Gillum, and Don E. Norton, Salt Lake City, Utah: Deseret Book Company; Provo, Utah: Foundation for Ancient Research and Mormon Studies, 1986, p. 82–83.

Nobel Prize, 1959, http://www.nobelprize.org/nobel_prizes/physics/laureates/1959/chamberlain-facts.html

Nobel Prize, 1995, https://www.nobelprize.org/nobel_prizes/physics/laureates/1995/press.html

Paul, Erich R., 1992, Science, Religion, and Mormon Cosmology: University of Illinois Press, 272 pp. ISBN 978-0-252-01895-4

Perlmutter, S.; Aldering, G.; Della Valle, M.; Deustua, S.; Ellis, R. S.; Fabbro, S.; Fruchter, A.; Goldhaber, G.; Goobar, A.; Groom, D. E.; Hook, I. M.; Kim, A. G.; Kim, M. Y.; Knop, R. A.; Lidman, C.; McMahon, R.

G.; Nugent, P.; Pain, R.; Panagia, N.; Pennypacker, C. R.; Ruiz-Lapuente, P.; Schaefer, B.; Walton, N., 1997, Discovery of a Supernova Explosion at Half the Age of the Universe and its Cosmological Implications: Lawrence Berkeley National Laboratory, Report LBNL-41172, 18 pp. http://www.osti.gov/accomplishments/documents/fullText/ACC04 26.pdf

Peterson, Daniel C, 2018, A preliminary note on the Bahá'í Faith: Sic et Non blog (https://www.patheos.com/blogs/danpeterson/2018/08/a-preliminary-note-on-the-bahai-faith.html).

Philby, H. StJ. B., 1933, The Empty Quarter: Henry Holt, New York, 432 pp.

Phillips, Walter Alison, 1911, Faust: Encyclopædia Britannica (11th ed.). Cambridge University Press. (no ISBN; see also https://en.wikipedia.org/wiki/Goethe%27s_Faust)

Pickrell, John, 2006, Timeline – Human Evolution: New Scientist, https://www.newscientist.com/article/dn9989-timeline-human-evolution/

Pinker, Steven, 2011, The better angels of our nature: Viking Books, 832 pp. ISBN 978-0-670-02295-3

Popper, Karl, 1959, The Logic of Scientific Discovery: Routledge Classics, 544 pp. ISBN 0-415-27843-0

Randall, Lisa, 2005, Warped Passages – unraveling the mysteries of the universe's hidden dimensions: Harper Perennial, 500 pp. ISBN 978-0-06-053109-6

Read, Max, 2018, How Much of the Internet Is Fake? Turns Out, a Lot of It, Actually: New York magazine, Dec. 26, 2018, http://nymag.com/intelligencer/2018/12/how-much-of-the-internet-is-fake.html

Renan, Joseph, 1890, The History of the Origins of Christianity, Book IV, The Antichrist: Mathieson & Company, p. 60–75.

Reu, M., 1944, Luther and the Scriptures: Wartburg Press, Columbus, Ohio, 23 pp.

Riess, Adam G.; Alexei V. Filippenko; Peter Challis; Alejandro Clocchiattia; Alan Diercks; Peter M. Garnavich; Ron L. Gilliland; Craig J. Hogan; Saurabh Jha; Robert P. Kirshner; B. Leibundgut; M. M. Phillips; David Reiss; Brian P. Schmidt; Robert A. Schommer; R. Chris Smith; J. Spyromilio; Christopher Stubbs; Nicholas B. Suntzeff; and John Tonry, 1998, Observational Evidence from Supernovae for an Accelerating Universe and a Cosmological Constant: Astrophysics, arXiv:astro-ph/9805201, 36 pp. doi:10.1086/300499

Riess, Adam G.; Macri, Lucas M.; Hoffmann, Samantha L.; Scolnic, Dan; Casertano, Stefano; Filippenko, Alexei V.; Tucker, Brad E.; Reid, Mark J.; Jones, David O., 2016, A 2.4% determination of the local value of the Hubble constant: doi:10.3847/0004-637X/826/1/56.

Robock, Alan, 2011, Nuclear winter is a real and present danger: Nature 473, p. 275–276 (19 May 2011) doi:10.1038/473275a.

Rodin, L.E.; and N.I. Bazilevich, 1968, Production and Mineral Cycling in Terrestrial Vegetation. Transl. ed. by G.E. Fogg. Edinburgh: Oliver and Boyd, 288 pp.

Russell, Bertrand; and Copleston, F.C., 1964, The Existence of God, in: The Existence of God, ed. with an Introduction by John Hick, Problems of Philosophy Series (New York: Macmillan), p. 175. ISBN 978-0020854500

Ryan, W.B.F. et al., 1997, An Abrupt Drowning of The Black Sea Shelf: Marine Geology 138. p. 119–126. doi:10.1016/S0025-3227(97)00007-8.

Ryther, J.H., 1963, Geographic variations in productivity. In: The Sea, London: Interscience, 2, pp. 347-380.

Satake, K., and B. Atwater, 2007, Long-Term Perspectives on Giant Earthquakes and Tsunamis at Subduction Zones (PDF): Annual Review of Earth and Planetary Sciences, Annual Reviews, 35: 351, doi:10.1146/annurev.earth.35.031306.140302

Schram, Stuart, 2007, Mao – the Unknown Story: The China Quarterly 189, March 2007, p. 205-208. doi:10.1017/S030574100600107X

Schultz, Cheryl B.; Cheryl Russell; and Louise Wynn, 2013, Restoration, Reintroduction, and captive Propagation for at-risk Butterflies: A review of British and American Conservation Efforts: Israel Journal of Ecology & Evolution 54, No., p. 41-61 1 doi:10.1560/IJEE.54.1.41

Sigurdsson, Haraldur; Kelley, Simon P; Leckie, R Mark; Carey, Steven N; Bralower, Timothy J; King, John W., 2000, History of circum-Caribbean explosive volcanism: $^{40}Ar/^{39}Ar$ Dating of Tephra Layers: Proceedings of the Ocean Drilling Program, Scientific Results 165 (2000): p. 299-314. doi:10.2973/odp.proc.sr.165.021.2000

Silver, Nate, 2012, The signal and the noise: Penguin, 534 pp. ISBN 978-1-59-420411-1

Smith, C.W.; and H. Richard Blank, 1979, Ancient mines of the Farah Garan area, southwestern Saudi Arabia: USGS Open-File Report 79-1659 https://pubs.er.usgs.gov/publication/ofr791659

Smith, Nathan D.; Jake R. Crandall; Spencer M. Hellert; William R. Hammer; and Peter J. Makovicky, 2011, Anatomy and affinities of large archosauromorphs from the lower Fremouw Formation (Early Triassic) of Antarctica: Journal of Vertebrate Paleontology, 31:4, p. 784-797. doi:10.1080/02724634.2011.

Smolin, Lee, 2006, The Trouble With Physics – The Rise of String Theory, The Fall of a Science, and What Comes Next: Houghton Mifflin Company, 392 pp. ISBN 13: 978-0-618-55105-7

Sorenson, John L., 1984, Digging into the Book of Mormon: Our Changing Understanding of Ancient America and Its Scripture, https://www.lds.org/ensign/1984/09/digging-into-the-book-of-mormon-our-changing-understanding-of-ancient-america-and-its-scripture?lang=eng

Sorenson, John L., 1985, An Ancient American Setting for the Book of Mormon: Deseret Books, Salt Lake City, Utah. 415 pp. ISBN 978-1-57-345157-4

Sorenson, John L., 1992, I have a question: Ensign, September 1992, https://www.lds.org/ensign/1992/09/i-have-a-question?lang=eng

Stein, Seth; and Emile A. Okal, 2011, The size of the 2011 Tohoku earthquake need not have been a surprise: EOS, Transactions of the American Geophysical Union 92, p. 227–228 (5 July 2011 issue), doi:10.1029/2011EO270005

Stephens, Trent D.; and D. Jeffrey Meldrum, with Forrest B. Peterson, 2001, Evolution and Mormonism: A Quest for Understanding: Signature Books, 250 pp. ISBN 1-56085-142-2

Strickland, J. D. H., 1965, Production of organic matter in the primary stages of the marine food chain. In: Chemical Oceanography. London and New York: Academic Press, 1, pp. 477-610.

Stubbs, Brian D., 2016, Changes in Languages from Nephi to Now: Four Corners Digital Design, Blanding, UT, 210 pp., ISBN 978-0-9914741-1-0

Talmage, James E., 1909(2014), The Great Apostasy: Steed Publishing, 176 pp., ISBN 978-1-467-97730-2

Thesiger, Wilfred, 1959, Arabian Sands: Penguin Books, London, 347 pp. ISBN 978-0-141-02549-0

Thompson, R.S., 1990, Late Quaternary vegetation and climate in the Great Basin, in: Betancourt, J.L., Van Devender, T.R., and Martin, P.S., Packrat middens; The last 40,000 years of biotic change: Tucson, AZ, The University of Arizona Press, p. 200-239. ISBN 978-0-8165-3284-1

Valley, John W.; Aaron J. Cavosie; Takayuki Ushikubo; David A. Reinhard; Daniel F. Lawrence; David J. Larson; Peter H. Clifton; Thomas F. Kelly; Simon A. Wilde; Desmond E. Moser; and Michael J. Spicuzza, 2014, Hadean age for a post-magma-ocean zircon confirmed by atom-probe tomography, Nature Geoscience 7, p. 219–223. doi:10.1038/ngeo2075 http://www.nature.com/ngeo/journal/vaop/ncurrent/full/ngeo2075.html

Virgil, The Aeneid, Book VI. http://classics.mit.edu/Virgil/aeneid.6.vi.html

Voss, David, 1999, 'New Physics' Finds a Haven at the Patent Office: Science, 284 (5418): 1252, doi:10.1126/science.284.5418.1252

Waitt, Richard, 2015, In the Path of Destruction: Washington State University Press, 413 pp. ISBN 978-0-874-22323-1

Welch, John W, 1969, Chiasmus in the Book of Mormon: BYU Studies 10 (1): 69–84.

Welsh, John W., 1981, Chiasmus in Antiquity: Structures, Analyses, Exegesis: Gerstenburg, 353 pp. ISBN 978-3806707977

Widtsoe, John A., 1908, Joseph Smith as a Scientist: Kessinger Publishing, 180 pp. ISBN: 978-1-605-97139-1

Whittaker, R.H., 1975, Communities and Ecosystems, Second Edition: Macmillan, London, 352 pp. ISBN 978-0-024-27390-1

Woit, Peter, 2006, Not Even Wrong: The Failure of String Theory and the Search for Unity in Physical Law: Basic Books, 291 pp. ISBN 13: 978-0-465-09275-8

Wynn, Jeffrey C; and H. Richard Blank, 1979, A preliminary assessment of the 1977 INPUT survey on the Arabian Shield, Kingdom of Saudi Arabia, with guides for interpretation and ground follow-up: USGS Open-File Report 79-1508 https://pubs.er.usgs.gov/publication/ofr791508

Wynn, Jeff; Adam Mosbrucker; Herbert Pierce; and Kurt R. Spicer, 2016, Where is the hot rock and where is the ground water – Using CSAMT to map beneath and around Mount St. Helens: Journal of Environmental & Engineering Geophysics 21, p. 79-87 http://dx.doi.org/10.2113/JEEG21.2.79

Wynn, Jeff; Herbert A. Pierce, 2015, Mount St. Helens: Controlled-source audio-frequency magnetotelluric (CSAMT) data and inversions: USGS Data Series 901 (HTML) https://pubs.er.usgs.gov/publication/ds901

Wynn, Jeff; Mike Williamson; and John Fleming, 2012, Induced polarization for subseafloor and deep ocean mapping: Sea Technology

Magazine, Sept 2012 issue, p. 47-50.
https://www.academia.edu/3986933/Induced_polarization_for_s
ub-seafloor_deep_ocean_oil_mapping

Wynn, Jeff, 2006, Mapping Ground Water in Three Dimensions -- An
Analysis of Airborne Geophysical Surveys of the Upper San Pedro
River Basin, Cochise County, Southeastern Arizona: USGS
Professional Paper 1674, 33 pp, 2 Plates
http://pubs.usgs.gov/pp/2006/1674/

Wynn, Jeff, Greta J. Orris, Pamela Dunlap, Mark D. Cocker, James D. Bliss,
2016, Geology and undiscovered resource assessment of the
potash-bearing Central Asia Salt Basin, Turkmenistan, Uzbekistan,
Tajikistan, and Afghanistan: Chapter AA in Global mineral resource
assessment: USGS Scientific Investigations Report 2010-5090-AA,
107 pp, 35 figures. doi:10.3133/sir20105090AA

Wynn, J.C., and Fleming, J.A., 2012, Seawater capacitance – a promising
proxy for mapping and characterizing drifting hydrocarbon plumes
in the deep ocean: Ocean Science, 8, p. 1099-1104.
http://www.ocean-sci.net/8/1099/2012/os-8-1099-2012.pdf

Wynn, Jeffrey C., and Shoemaker, Eugene M., 1998, The Day the Sands
Caught Fire: Scientific American 279, (5), p. 36-45 (November
1998 issue) http://volcanoes.usgs.gov/jwynn/1998SciAm-
Wabar.pdf

Wynn, J.C., 2002a, Mapping Armageddon with a magnetometer – the Wabar
impact site at 61ºC: Proceedings of the Environmental &
Engineering Geophysical Society, Las Vegas, NV, February 10-14,
14 pp. http://library.seg.org/doi/pdf/10.4133/1.2927080

Wynn, J.C., 2002b, Mapping an iron meteorite impact site with a
magnetometer, and implications for the probability of a
catastrophic impact on Earth: Journal of Environmental &
Engineering Geophysics, 7, no. 4 (December 2002), p. 143-150.
doi:10.4133/JEEG7.4.143.

Wynn, Louise, Jason Held, Akos Kereszturi, and Judd Reed, J., 2004, The
Geophysical Study Of An Earth Impact Crater As An Analogue For
Studying Martian Impact Craters in: On To Mars 2: edited by
Zubrin, R.M., and Crossman, F.: Collector's Guide Publishing Inc.,
6 pp., 2006 ed. doi:10.1.1.659.7026

Zahnle, Kevin, Nick Arndt, Charles Cockell, Alex Halliday, Euan Nisbet,
Franck Selsis, and Norman H. Sleep, 2007, Emergence of a
Habitable Planet: Space Sciences Reviews 129, p. 35–78.
doi:10.1007/s11214-007-9225-z

Acknowledgments

This book was started by a kind answer from Dan Peterson, a professor in the Department of Asian and Near Eastern Languages at Brigham Young University. It has been substantially revised and improved following draft reviews by Maurice McBride (an energy security legal advisor in the Middle East), Don and Kathleen Lind (NASA astronaut, retired), and David Grant (More Good Foundation).

Our daughter Lisa, a professor and department chair at Macquarie University in Sydney, Australia, gave the draft text its most ferocious and thorough editing. When we teach Jujitsu together there is always a perhaps not surprising payback: we learn subtle new things *from our students*. Likewise, when we raise and teach our children and then begin to learn *from* them, then it seems like this meets Plato's definition of a successful life. In that Platonic sense, we have lived a very successful life – and we're very proud of all five of them (and their partners).

Please note, however, that any errors are attributable only to us, not to anyone else who reviewed this book.

The Authors

Louise was born into a Church family. As a teenager she started thinking about the Church and Christianity and religion in general, thus beginning what would be a lifelong testing process that went hand in hand with her later studies and advanced degrees in linguistics and environmental science. More important than her formal degrees, though, have been her reading and studying on her own and discussing gospel principles with informed members of the Church in all kinds of settings, on three continents.

Jeff got there by following a very different path. He was raised a Catholic but became an atheist somewhere between 11 and 12 years old. Until he was 15, in fact, he was a Catholic Atheist Altar-Boy because his mother dragged him to church with her. By college he had evolved into an arrogant, militant, abrasive atheist. You've probably met the type.

In his junior year as a physics major at Berkeley, Jeff realized that the belief system of an atheist had at least as many holes and unproven assumptions – and fewer explanations – than the belief system of any adherent of faith. Explain the Anthropic Principle, or what preceded the Big Bang? The un-provable idea of a multiverse? That won't even pass for a theory, much less a scientific hypothesis. It's untestable, so by definition is not even science.

So which is the more assumptive, i.e., "non-scientific" belief system?

Years earlier a friend joined the Church of Jesus Christ. Hmmm. That's interesting, Jeff thought. Two years later Jim's girlfriend (now his wife Nancy) joined, and Jeff asked her why. The answer was a real attention-getter: *because you can test if it is true.*

You can test it. That's one sure way to get the attention of a scientist.

Together, we once heard a friend compare this experience to taking a teaspoonful of honey, and feeling the warm glow suffuse through your entire body. Subsequently we learned of how closely 1 Nephi describes the Frankincense Trail. There are sentences there that only a Semitic language speaker who herded goats and lived among Bedouin could have possibly written. As chief scientist for volcano hazards with the US Geological Survey, Jeff was astounded to learn how closely 3 Nephi 8 describes a subduction-margin volcano-tectonic event one or two orders of magnitude greater than the 1980 eruption of Mount St Helens. Central America is chock full of geologic evidence of much larger such events – including two super-volcano eruptions (Chiltepe and Masaya) that neatly bracket Christ's death in the eastern hemisphere. From Brian Stubbs we have learned how the Uto-Aztecan language group has over 1,500 cognates with ancient central Arabian Semitic languages – an astonishing link. None of this information was available to a 23-yr-old with a 3rd grade education, living on the rural frontier of New York State in 1828. There are lots of others, but we have direct personal experience with these.

As we have both grown older, we have had many, many "coincidences" happen. The aggregate of all of them, however, is something that we at least can no longer argue with. Among other things, we've both had unusual success in careers as scientist-scholars – opportunity after opportunity has opened, and we have never had to waste time knocking around in a dead-end research path. Some of these miracles were small, some were just blow-down astonishing, but together they make a compelling, cumulative pattern. It's like flipping a coin and it always comes up heads... after a while the accumulating odds show that some subtle intervention must be going on. None of these, alone by itself, violated our free agency. However, the aggregate of all these miracles, and answers to prayers have become so overwhelming that neither of us could anymore deny our faith. We would have to ignore our entire previous life experiences to do so.

We once listened together to Don Lind (NASA Astronaut) as he gave a lecture at the University of Arizona. Don had earned a PhD in high-energy physics from Berkeley. In that lecture he made an interesting point, which we paraphrase here: *'This is the only religion that I can follow and not have to believe one thing on Sunday and something else the rest of the week. This is the only religion I can adhere to as a scientist.'*

I suppose this is why we use the word "Amen."

Yes! Exactly.

Figure 4. Jeff with the "Cookie Monster", south of Pu'u O'o, and southeast of Kilauea Volcano, Big Island of Hawai'i.

Figure 5. Louise near the Mars Society Flashline Observatory, Haughton Impact Crater, Devon Island, Nunavut Province, Canadian High Arctic, where she served as mission scientist.

Made in the USA
Monee, IL
24 October 2022